Only You Can Help Yourself

One Wrong Note

Ann Lawson

chipmunkapublishing
the mental health publisher

Ann Lawson

Published by
Chipmunkapublishing
PO Box 6872
Brentwood
Essex CM13 1ZT
United Kingdom

http://www.chipmunkapublishing.com

Chipmunkapublishing gratefully acknowledge the support of Arts Council England.

Only You Can Cure Yourself

This is a blog I wrote on Yahoo360 for three years during my recovery. Yahoo360 is now closing on the Internet so I wanted to preserve it as I think it makes a good story.

Entry for May 30, 2006

Pissing down with rain; cruel, sharp and formidable. Wondering whether to pay my next instalment of council tax. .... Just paid it on line.

In Italy they say you learn seven things every day. I stayed in Carrara, where the marble comes from, when I was a teenager with an aristocratic family who were very sweet to me. I loved it. I answered an ad in the back of the Times. They wanted someone to teach English. Then when I was 19 after my A levels my parents sent me for a holiday with some family friends, but I totally misunderstood the situation and thought it was another job. When I flew to my grandparents in Italy afterwards there was a terrible car crash that morning and my Italian suitor was killed. I knew, then, nothing would ever be the same again.

Then four years ago my mother told me the name of the French people I was staying with and I realised I had made a mistake. I am now 55

Entry for May 30, 2006

Pissing down with rain. Cruel, sharp and formidable. Wondering whether to pay my next instalment of council tax. .... Just paid it on line. In Italy they say you learn seven things every day. I stayed in Carrara where the marble comes from when I was a teenager with an aristocratic family who were very sweet to me. I loved it. I answered an ad in the back of the Times. They wanted someone to teach English. Then when I was 19, after my A levels, my parents sent me to France for a holiday with some family friends, but I totally misunderstood the situation and thought it was another job. When I flew to my grandparents in Italy afterwards there was a car crash that morning and my Italian boyfriend was killed. I knew then, nothing would be the same again. Then four years ago my mother told me the name of the French people I was staying with

3

and I realised I had made a mistake. I am now 55. I have a daughter of 23 called Tanya Francella. I wanted to call her Tristelle. She is travelling at the moment and has met a Dutch man called Reinier. Tomorrow I have some reading matter and music arriving from amazon.com. Also my new man is coming over. I say new but we know each other very well after just two months. He is called Chris. He is a retired further education physics teacher. He is waiting for his decree absolute. He has a son who has Asperger's syndrome, called David. The French family I stayed with had one member who got the Nobel Prize for physics: Louis de Broglie. Augustin de Broglie stayed on our farm as a student when I was a child and I remember him well. I was supposed to go to Oxford University after France but I failed my entrance. My brother went to Oxford and died with a knife in his heart in the middle of the night. My father also went to Oxford (Balliol College) but he keeps very quiet about that now. My sister and her family are coming over from New Zealand this Christmas. I am on section 17 leave from mental hospital and not allowed to drive. The rain has stopped temporarily. I have some trouble with my feet. I enjoy smoking. I don't think the two are connected.   :-)   I'll keep you posted......
There were five children in our family Ruth, Ann (me), Roger (who died), Adrian and Robert. Now I think I'll phone Chris. I'd like to go to Paris again soon.

Entry for September 02, 2006

It takes me a long while to wake up these days. My mood doesn't usually lift till quite late on. I may be up at 7.30 or 8.00 but, if I have no pressing matters, I'm not bathed and dressed till midday. Ah well! It is Saturday and it's raining. My parents fly to Montenegro today for a long delayed holiday after my father's hip replacement. I was going to Holt today to see Chris but he said last night he wanted to come and see me in Norwich. So I'm expecting him in half and hour.

Entry for October 02, 2006

Wide awake and it's nearly one in the morning. Chris my fella is in New York, staying with his sister till next Monday. I'm feeling great. I have three afternoon's work this week and Mum is coming to see me on Wednesday. I am picking up little bargains from the charity shop I work in all the time and am pleased with nearly all my small purchases. I even got a Microsoft keyboard for a pound the other day.

Dad is back playing golf after his hip operation and everything seems much more cheerful at home. I'm keeping fit too without a car. I went swimming at the university with my friend Diane last Sunday for 3/4 of an hour. Today I walked to the doctor's and also walked back from work. I have the blisters to show for it. I will apply for a new driving license when I am allowed to in November but I am increasingly thinking that I won't get a new car yet. You meet so many more people without a car, just using the buses. I'm also becoming less agoraphobic.

I see so much progress in my life all the time that the contrast with how depressed and hurt I used to feel is terrific. And yet I have kept all my old mental health friends - well the ones I like. Mum says life is swings and roundabouts but I think it is more of a climb and the view gets better every day.

The shrink I am under now has agreed to reduce my medication over a 5-month period to the lowest possible dosage. After that we will reassess. At the moment I can live with the situation and even think some times the medication may be helping, although that thought is a little far fetched. I only have to see the community psychiatric nurse once a fortnight and have absolutely no other contact. It's almost like freedom. The dreaded social worker is totally out of the picture.

I haven't heard from my daughter for quite a while now. She is of course travelling. Everyone has written to her, with no reply forthcoming. We don't even know what continent she is on. I'm pretty relaxed about it though and it gives me a chance to develop my life, which is all she ever wanted for

I am very pleased about the anti-age discrimination legislation, which has come in and immediately applied for a new job (paid) interviewing first time passport applicants to establish the veracity of their identity.

Ann Lawson

The photo was taken on Aldeburgh beach this summer by Chris, (Benjamin Britten country) where my parents live. I am very pleased with the way Chris and my relationship is going. We have been getting on well since last February and I am very happy. It's a lot of work and a lot of pleasure too. The work mostly consists of cooking, which I am getting very good at. The pleasure is walking and seeing the sights and pavement cafe chilling and taking rattling old buses out to the country to visit him. He's a bright lad, courteous, considerate and has a lot of go for someone 8 years older than me.

Socrates said the unexamined life is not worth living. I don't think that is generally true, but certainly before I had the absolute humility and dedication to really examine my life and discover the truth of what had been bothering me my life wasn't worth living either. Now it is as rich a tapestry as anyone could desire and getting better all the time. Life isn't a bed of roses but neither is it torment upon torment. My recovery has been very slow but now I'm making progress and have been for 3 or 4 years now I have everything to live for. And I have absolute confidence I am over the fundamental flaw that was holding me back. My tutor on the on-line philosophy course I am doing congratulated me on my achievement in self-analysis; the first person who has. But as I replied, the rewards it has brought are enough to make me very happy without congratulations. It was the hardest thing I have ever done but I did it and I am no longer mentally ill. That is such an achievement after 35 years in Stygian gloom I'd like to shout it from the rooftops. But of course then they would think I am high ;) I just hope it encourages others to see that there can be an end to torment.

Entry for October 31, 2006

Well today is Hallowe'en. We have had so much abuse and vandalism from the kids round here this last year I don't think I'll be participating. In fact Chris is coming over specially in order to give me some support in case it gets out of hand.

The big news is that my daughter, who was travelling round the world, phoned me a couple of weeks ago to say she has come to settle in Norwich; so we are all relieved to know she is safe. She hasn't actually shown her face to me yet or revealed her address but she is working and her boyfriend Reinier will soon be working and they are renting a flat.

Even Randy Andy is back in touch, so things are good.

This article was written before I felt better and widely disseminated on the web and very well received.

Only You Can Cure Yourself
By Ann Lawson
Norwich, UK

Mental illness has an extremely poor image. It's been called the last taboo. Unfortunately those who suffer or have suffered from being diagnosed with a mental illness tend to be dragged down by this image. Once you have been diagnosed or initially admitted to an institution for treatment, it is almost impossible to escape the stigmatisation, which automatically follows. Nor is it only those on the outside of the caring professions who carry these prejudices. Blind ignorance is also rife within psychiatry. There is currently a research article, which connects schizophrenia to the incidence of being cross-eyed or being born in a month with particularly intemperate weather. It seems we have progressed little from when entrails were read in Ancient Rome to anticipate events. The fact is no one has a clue about what causes schizophrenia, although as with most things these days a genetic cause is being sought, so far with little success. The most widely held theory for nearly all kinds of mental illness is it is due to a chemical imbalance in the brain.

I find this fascinating since no patient these days avoids the use of chemicals from first diagnosis, often till death. So how do psychiatrists determine that there is a chemical imbalance when the brains of mental patients have been bombarded with powerful chemicals from the beginning? What is even more disturbing about this theory is that if the drugs themselves have caused this imbalance, is that not good reason for stopping them?

Psychiatric drugs do not in any way cure the patient or even make him or her feel better. The side effects are appalling. They include the onset of neurological disorders. These include diabetes due to weight gain and innumerable minor and not so minor discomforts. It is seldom claimed that the drugs are therapeutic: They merely mask symptoms – symptoms, which probably were less troubling than the effects of the drugs. The drugs do this by crudely interfering with the normal chemical makeup of the brain, making thought processes difficult and sleep hard to avoid. Did you ever wonder why mental patients are like zombies? Well, there's your answer. Psychiatric drugs are making them feel ill and cause them to see the world with only half a brain. Drugs are the current historical sequel to long term institutionalisation and chains - and lobotomy. Basically psychiatry is a violent and intrusive way of controlling people who do not conform to other people's expectations - or those who are vulnerable. Remember that treatment is not voluntary once force is used. Mental patients do not have meaningful civil rights. In the UK, often they are not even allowed to vote. In "hospitals," "medication" is routinely administered by force if the patient refuses or is "non-compliant". Mental patients have no right to privacy even when living in the community: "Health" workers may go round neighbours asking about the "patient's" behaviour, among other ploys. Medication is usually administered for a lifetime. There is no way anyone ever gets 'better' on psychiatric drugs. Being 'mentally ill' is a social status, not a medical condition. And the hospitals are merely prisons.

Why has psychiatry not been abandoned, since it is based on overt ignorance and involves obvious abuse? Why does the myth of mental illness persist?

Of course, we all suffer from time to time - usually depression resulting from life experience. There are various strategies, which can be used to lift ones spirits and improve one's health. They include exercise and diet. However the idea of the mentally ill as a category of persons distinct from the rest of the human race continues. I think this happens partly because of vested interests: The companies that market the drugs, which are the current treatment, make vast profits exceeded only by share prices for Internet companies. It is in the interest of these drug companies and their shareholders, which include many doctors, that psychiatry widen its net, constantly bringing more and more people into the sphere of those who are forced to ingest psychiatric drugs for the rest of their lives. Their motives and their lack of a sense of social responsibility are like those of the tobacco companies.

A drug has recently been developed which makes people less shy. Suddenly a new illness, a new diagnosis, was created to make use of this drug: "social phobia." Now people are being diagnosed with this and - surprise! Surprise! - are prescribed this new drug. The need to sell this drug and make a profit actually created the diagnosis! Tobacco companies do not need to force their customers to smoke since tobacco is highly addictive. Most people find psychiatric drugs almost intolerable. So drug advocates create such fear and paranoia concerning mentally ill people (who are statistically considerably less dangerous to others than the general population) that a hysterical policy of containment and pharmacological control of mental patients is adopted and enforced.

Some researchers search for the causes of mental illness, particularly schizophrenia, ad infinitum. Science is no where nearer to understanding it than when it was first defined. Based on considerable experience and with great confidence, I argue that the whole course of this "illness" is created by the way it is "treated." It is the confinement, the stigmatisation, the ignorance, the physical and emotional abuse, the drugs, the prejudice of employers and consequent poverty, and the overbearing attitude of psychiatrists and others that cause this "illness." For most people, mental illness has a career path from which there is no escape. There is a vast industry profiting financially from the abject misery of mental patients whose problems are exacerbated by an effort to create hysteria, thereby making them outcasts. This makes sense of the otherwise cruel and senseless profession of psychiatry. The mentally ill are an essential part of what supports a very profitable psychiatric drug manufacturing industry. And psychiatry maintains the status quo by drugging into oblivion those who challenge it.

I'm not saying there are not vulnerable individuals, individuals with problems, and unhappy people - even people who are not healthy. But I am saying that conventional western psychiatry does not even attempt to cure them but simply to contain them and perpetuate them as "patients." Secondly, western psychiatry often creates problems, such as in the case of schizophrenia, where there were none before, by its attitude and its "treatment." The widening grip of psychiatry also has been at the expense of less intrusive, more friendly and wholesome approaches to helping mentally or emotionally troubled people. What might be a temporary problem due to some minor upset or even a mistaken diagnosis, psychiatry can and usually does convert into a dramatic condition, which requires a lifetime of treatment. This damages the individual to the core of his being. The mentally ill are not more dangerous than anyone else despite the way they are mistreated. Paranoid schizophrenia is a logical response to psychiatric treatment and not the result of some unfortunate genetic modification. Any fool should be able to understand this, but try explaining it to a psychiatrist! It makes more sense to them what the temperature was outside when you were born. Who is mad here - the patients or the doctors?

Ann Lawson

Sequel to 'Only You Can Cure Yourself'

Ann Lawson, Norwich 2006

My first article was very well received about the need for the individual to grasp their psychiatric illness by the horns and shake it till the truth came out. I was still ill when I wrote that but taking my own advice, shortly afterwards I was able to tease out, although with immense effort and embarrassing humility, the key to my own illness. I had looked everywhere for the cause of my illness. Therapy makes you do that. You put your life under a microscope. You tear your life and other people's lives apart trying to find out why you became ill. Your confidence hits rock bottom and you despair of ever getting out of the mire.

I had some time to my self and access to a telephone and also a guide; my daughter had been in therapy and identified the main problem, as me not getting on with my parents. So I really worked on this and gave it all my effort. It was a short trip to madness and back. I was only trying to help my daughter and would, as all parents, do anything for her. So I put my reputation on the line and bombarded my parents with questions. Before that I had always been running away from them and my problems and the mental health services. It required about three weeks of concerted effort, fumbling in the dark, with no one to guide me but the dark mess of my mind. The pay off has been beyond my wildest dreams. I learnt that I had made a major mistake in 1969 and I learnt that my parents loved me more dearly than I had ever imagined.

My first piece of creative writing was saying mental illness is like travelling through East Anglia during the war when all the road signs were taken down to prevent a German invasion. I didn't know where I was going, except as far from my parents as possible to start a new life without mental health services and the reputation my parents had given me by repeated hospitalisations. It was a constant cat and mouse game, which I always seemed to lose. I begged to be left alone and be respected for the person I was however flawed. But the net just got tighter and tighter. Life also became more and more dangerous and unhappy. But, unlike some people, I did have a benchmark from a time when things were good and also the fortune that both my parents were still alive.

I had left home at 19 after a difficult time and made my own life, even gone to university. But that life unravelled without my parents support and I nearly had a full- blown breakdown at university. I soldiered on and after getting a mediocre degree moved to the north of England to live and work. I then came home, as I thought temporarily, found myself, pregnant and had an abortion. Then I got a job as a social worker in Norwich and a flat in the city.

It was then the powers of 'normality' stepped in and had me admitted to mental hospital. I soon realised the hospital was just a holding centre for miscreants with no progress possible and nothing to do but take drugs. I discharged myself after a week. Then the horror struck because my brother who had been studying at Oxford was found by his housemates one midday when he didn't turn up for lectures dead in bed with a knife in his heart.

Life stopped. Empty out the oceans and sweep up the woods. Pack up the stars; put away the sun and the moon they are not needed anymore. Nothing shall come to any good now. To my parents Roger was their east their west their north their south their Sunday best. The first- born boy.

If I hadn't been ill I don't think Roger would have killed himself. We are a family of high achievers. Perhaps Roger couldn't bear the thought that his elder sister had been put in mental hospital. Perhaps my illness had affected him more deeply than I had known. Perhaps without the aggressive intervention of the local country doctor who had me first admitted (out of the blue so it seemed to me) Roger's death would not have been precipitated. I might have been able to work out my problems peacefully and much earlier. Who can tell? Certainly I have always found medical intervention terribly disruptive of thought and life.

After that for the next thirty years I suffered admission after admission. I hated it so much I even committed arson hoping to go to prison rather than mental hospital. I nearly ended up in Broadmoor secure hospital on that occasion. I was desperately unhappy and often in grave danger. I have no idea how many times I tried to kill myself or even how many times I was admitted to hospital. Life in hospital was like watching paint dry on most occasions but I was conscious there was a bit missing in my psychological make up. Euthanasia would have been a blessing.

Then I became pregnant again. The abortion clinic had advised me this might happen and I decided to keep the child and vowed to stand by her forever. She was such a tiny bundle of life and happiness I was ecstatic for a while. But the social services and mental health authorities and my parents spent little time in claiming her for their own and I soon learnt I was a mother in name alone and she wasn't mine to love, hold and adore. But I continued to do so against all odds even when they finally succeeded in putting her in care when she was about 12. When she went to university the social services went to court to prevent me having her address and I reached such a point of anxiety I thought she was dead, in all honesty.

Now I know I don't have to battle so hard unless provoked and that God, whatever you conceive him to be, looks after his own. I know now that in 1969 my parents were opening out a new vista for me not consigning me to a humdrum job. It was a rite of passage, which I failed to understand. I too would have gone to Oxford if I had had the information I have now. They sent me to France to stay with a family called the de Broglies who I knew from when their sons had stayed on our farm as students when we were younger. But in 1969 my family failed to tell me the name of the family I was staying with so I never put 2 and 2 together. I thought I was a humble servant for some snotty French family dad had sold some pigs to. In fact I was a family friend, to a family with an aristocratic pedigree, one of who was a Nobel Prize winner. To find out the truth was like coming home. It was at my daughter's suggestion I badgered and badgered Mum and Dad to find the truth, but the pay off is worth all the tea in China. It was a niggling confusion, but enough to trouble me, and my brother, to death.

I can't change the past. But I can live in the present knowing just how much my parents loved me, and that it is a good world, not one of endless graft as I thought before; one where love and liaisons matter; one where families, as proud as the de Broglies, are able to do favours for our family. One where I have a guardian angel. I thought it was only I enabling myself to survive. I had been battling against the world for so long the relief that what the world had wanted for me was even greater than I had ever hoped was to find joy.

The mental health authorities and the police have not accepted my change of heart and mind and still persecute me with sectioning at regular intervals. Nor am I off medication but, like the snail climbing out of the well, I may fall down 3 inches every night, but I climb up four inches every day. I am sad I have wasted so much of my life in deep unhappiness and the unhappiness I have caused others and I am sad I didn't achieve more. However the joy of not being at odds with your family and working towards a seamless whole is without peer.

Mental illness is the devil in disguise. I can't put it any stronger than that. Life is hard enough without having such a flaw in your character you come to the attention of the authorities. For all the numerous interventions I received it was only having the space and time and hard application to sort the problem out myself that enabled me to come through. See! I'm still alive and contributing now whereas before I would hide my light under a bushel because I knew I was wrong. I just didn't know where I had gone wrong. I have complete confidence in my own sanity now and hopefully other people will slowly come to realise that the pattern of the last thirty years has been broken. Life is no easier. In fact it is harder. But it is much more rewarding. And now I have that knowledge of what might have been, I can only try and achieve a little of my parents' vision in those years I have left. You can only cure yourself. But it's worth it. I now live in the real world and it's really not such a bad one.

Entry for February 04, 2007

Brahmanism: This is the sum of duty: Do naught unto others which would cause you pain if done to you: Mahabharata 5:1517

Christianity: All things whatsoever ye would that men should do to you, do ye even so to them: Matthew 7:12
Islam: No one of you is a believer until he desires for his brother what which he desires for himself. Sunnah

Buddhism: Hurt not others in ways that you yourself would find hurtful: Udana Varga 5:18

Judaism: What is hateful to you; do not to your fellowmen. That is the entire Law; all the rest is commentary: Talmud, Shabbat 31: a

Confucianism: Surely it is the maxim of loving-kindness: Do not unto others that you would not have them do unto you: Analects 15:23

Taoism: Regard your neighbour's gain as your own gain, and your neighbour's loss as your own loss: T'ai Shag Kan Ying P'ien

Zoroastrianism: That nature alone is good which refrains from doing unto another whatsoever is not good: for itself. : Dadistan-i-dinik 94:

Entry for November 07, 2006

Mum and Dad had two extra tickets for Madame Butterfly, the opera on Sunday and asked Chris and myself; we travelled to Ipswich by bus and train, but on arriving at Ipswich station, saw dad charging down the platform with blood on his face. Turned out he had just tripped over the pavement (He had a hip operation this year). So I went into the station master's office with him and we made an attempt to patch him up till a wonderful first aid lady arrived and soon he was presentable enough to go to the opera. We insisted we take a taxi and leave their car at the station.

The opera was great and I had no trouble sitting still for the duration, which is what I often find difficult. It's a sad, sad story. I have in fact seen it before but much of the music was new. We had some of the best seats in the house (a very dilapidated theatre) as dad's hearing isn't the best now.

Suddenly we realised we had no way home to the station but dad suggested we walk so with Dad charging ahead we all walked through the darkened streets back to the station, me accompanying Dad and Chris and Mum taking up the rear. We missed our train by a whisker so had an hour to wait on the station which was spent very enjoyably, warm as toast after our walk and all the station personnel curious to know how my father was since he had made quite an impression.

We got home about 1-2 in the morning, which would have been fine but Chris was up at 7.30 in the morning to go to Holt, and as I was working in the afternoon, I sort of sleep walked through the day. I spent yesterday in bed snoozing, the new sheets and mattress I brought recently are really comfortable.

Today I am going up to the city, I'm going to do my shopping and drop into Bridges the drop in centre for people with mental health problems and catch up on the news and have a coffee in the city. Chris has gone to London for a couple of days to see his son and his old mates.

November 19, 2006

This is Chris my best friend and lover.

I thought I'd update you on my daughter; she has been travelling after leaving university and selling her house in Manchester. She went to South Africa, India and Sri Lanka then back to South Africa to be with Reinier, a Dutch man she has met. I have been worried sick about her though she wrote some lovely e-mails about her adventures on safari and white water rafting and motor biking on quad bikes across the desert.

Then her e-mails stopped coming for a few months (we had a bit of an altercation on line) and I only got news third hand. Suddenly a month ago or so she phoned me out of the blue and told me she and Reinier had been living here in Norwich for the last month! Naturally I wanted to see her though Chris told me to play it cool and I phoned her a few times. But she didn't arrange anything. So after a month of mild depression I decided not to phone her till she phoned me. Hey presto! Last night she phoned to say Reinier has landed a job in Ireland with Apple Mac and they are moving to Ireland. Also she said she would be asking me over for a meal before they left. So it's all very exciting and has turned out well. Some times life seems so gloomy and unfair but then the sun shines again and everything is good. You just have to hang in there in the mean time. And also cultivate good friends because a friendly chat can ease the worst of worries. I often recite the desiderata to myself and it has seen me through many troubled times.

Max Ehrmann

Only You Can Cure Yourself

Desiderata

Go placidly amid the noise and haste,
and remember what peace there may be in silence.
As far as possible without surrender,
be on good terms with all persons.
Speak your truth quietly and clearly;
and listen to others,
even the dull and the ignorant;
they too have their story.

Avoid loud and aggressive persons,
they are vexations to the spirit.
If you compare yourself with others,
you may become vain and bitter;
for always there will be greater and lesser persons than yourself.
Enjoy your achievements as well as your plans.

Keep interested in your own career, however humble;
it is a real possession in the changing fortunes of time.
Exercise caution in your business affairs;
for the world is full of trickery.
But let this not blind you to what virtue there is;
many persons strive for high ideals;
and everywhere life is full of heroism.

Be yourself.
Especially, do not feign affection.
Neither be cynical about love;
for in the face of all aridity and disenchantment
it is as perennial as the grass.

Take kindly the counsel of the years,
gracefully surrendering the things of youth.
Nurture strength of spirit to shield you in sudden misfortune.
But do not distress yourself with dark imaginings.
Many fears are born of fatigue and loneliness.

Beyond a wholesome discipline,
be gentle with yourself.

You are a child of the universe,
no less than the trees and the stars;
you have a right to be here.
And whether or not it is clear to you,
no doubt the universe is unfolding as it should.

Therefore be at peace with God,
whatever you conceive Him to be,
and whatever your labours and aspirations,
in the noisy confusion of life keep peace with your soul.

With all its sham, drudgery, and broken dreams,
it is still a beautiful world.
Be cheerful.
Strive to be happy.

Max Ehrmann, Desiderata, Copyright 1952.

Entry for December 31, 2006

Only You Can Cure Yourself

This is a photo of me in November (I'm wearing a peace poppy) drinking tea in Eaton Park which is near my house, taken by Chris.

I haven't posted for a while so I am way behind with my news. Christmas was a blast. I made gentle and organised preparations, and then Chris and I took the train to Ipswich on the Sunday before, and Chris went on to stay with his ex -wife and son (who has Asperger's syndrome) in London and I took the train to Saxmundham in Suffolk and stayed with Mum and Dad and my sister and her family who were over from New Zealand in Aldeburgh. On Christmas day we all travelled to the farm at Stradbroke and my Canadian sister in law put on a meal for 16 including her parents. Her father had never met some of her five children so it was all very jolly and a super meal. There was a roaring wood fire and we opened the presents in the sitting room. My daughter phoned up in the middle of the meal from Ireland as she was the only member of the family who could not be with us and we put the call on loud speaker.

On Boxing Day Mum and Dad and my sister and her man went for a five-mile walk near Minsmere bird reserve. We took a picnic lunch.

Then on the Wednesday Chris came down by train to Saxmundham and we all had a drinks party and very nice buffet done by a professional firm at Mum and Dad's, so Chris has met my whole family now. That morning we all had a Christmas card and a lovely long letter from my daughter with all her news and an address for her so at last she is settled again in Ireland and we are in easy contact. Her man Reinier has a very good job with a pharmaceutical firm (Allergen) in Ireland so they have rented a house and will look round for somewhere to buy. They are in County Mayo. Chris and I will probably visit during the next year.

Oh and then yesterday guess what! My driving license arrived on the door- mat. It is a yearly renewable one but now I can look for a car and will be mobile again!! In fact I am loath to turn my back on public transport because we have had such fun using city and country buses and all for free! It's a whole new social life and not half as alienating as private transport where you are cocooned within your own car. It's not as stressful either.

Well Christmas didn't really kick off as everyone expected, amongst my friends, since I was spending it with my family. Despite the hoards of people it was really a lovely traditional Christmas with loads of good feelings. I did lose my temper with Mum at one point but then every one was grumbling about her, poor woman. It's just that I was the only one who sparked.

Today is New Year's Eve and Chris and I woke early. We have been chatting in bed and Chris is now reading and probably is ready for his third cup of tea. It is wonderful having someone to chat to and spend time with in a relaxed way. Perhaps I'll start the book my sister gave me for Christmas today. We are sure to go for a walk, although it is a bit dull out there.

Wishing all my friends a happy, healthy and prosperous New Year.

Entry for January 22, 2007

Well this is one form of transport, the north Norfolk railway. Here is the steam train at Sheringham. But I now have another form! I have my driving license back and have bought a little car or rather Ford

Ka! So I am mobile again. Funny thing is I woke up happy the morning my license arrived in the post even before I had opened it. I'm getting the hang of driving again. Naturally I'm a bit nervous after a year off the road.

Seven years continual recovery after 30 years of mental illness

Busting a gasket

I had a bad night last night. The only way I can control my deep unhappiness is to sleep and last night I didn't sleep a wink. It's not too serious as I sleep so much during the day but all sorts of problems were playing on my mind. Amongst these problems was the person who stopped the letter from my solicitor before my last sectioning which would have kept me from being sectioned if it had gone through. I presume it was my humourless new GP. I should have discussed it with Chris but at 1.30 I (wrongly) presumed he would be in bed asleep. So I lay awake all night and gradually thought about my family and by morning phoned Chris; but he thought it was his alarm and turned it off. So then I blasted each and everyone of my family down the phone. So several black marks for me to add to my store and further destruction of my freedom and reputation no doubt. All the family laughed out loud at me and said I was mad. So generally I feel as sick as a pig with them. They all have their wealthy cosy life styles and 'get at Ann' is a national sport. Anyway eventually I managed to discuss it with Chris and against his advice wrote to my GP.

So now I am in deep dodo, and can't expect any favours from anyone.

Life stinks

Saturday March 3, 2007 - 11:46am

Lots of good news!

The first bit of good news is that my daughter has finally passed her driving test on the fifth attempt. She flew over from Ireland and stayed in bed and breakfast and took it in Lowestoft where it is supposed to be easier. So it was great excitement all round! She has bought a little Fiat Punto and fixed a dog guard in the back for Lara and now is getting known as one of the slowest drivers in Ireland where she lives. It's great because she is in a country area so at last she can get out and about when Reinier is at work. We are going out to see them hopefully in June.

Second bit of good news is I finally had a holiday after so many cancellations due to ill health. Chris and I went to Italy courtesy of Ryan air and spent three days in Ancona, which is a big port half way down on the east coast. We booked coach tickets to Stansted and left at 3 in the morning. Everyone was worried because the news had made such a fuss about the snow, but it was only a smattering. When we arrived we had to wait for a bus into Ancona (about 10 kilometres) but we made it and found the hotel. It was very central, near the railway station and several small cafes and restaurants. We had booked everything over the net so the whole holiday came to less than £300 for both of us including spending money. And everything went like clockwork. Italy was mild and it was pleasant wandering around, deciphering bus timetables and watching the trains. We took a trolley car into the town and went round a terrific market, which included a covered area with wonderful fruit and vegetables and fish and meat including horsemeat. I discovered I had dropped my camera. So we asked for the nearest Carabinieri to report it and were entertained for some time by the military police (I had made a bit of a mistake we should have asked for the polizeii) who were wearing full regalia with helmets and white plumes and silver epaulettes and swords. They very cordially wrote a report for my insurance and even gave me a cough sweet.

Saturday we went out for a meal in a proper restaurant with white linen tables because Chris wanted spaghetti! I wasn't really hungry, because I had munched my way through half a salami earlier in the day. Chris had actually had two slices of pizza at an excellent fast food place near by, which cooked with oil rather than animal fat, so all the food was very healthy and light.

I found my Italian was well understood, and with the help of my dictionary and Chris's phrasebook we did very well. People were very helpful too. We had great fun watching Italian television in our room, especially the adverts for 'slim and lift', a corset of some kind which was getting the hard sell. I think mainly the holiday was about immersing ourselves in Italian life as it wasn't a beach or a beautiful scenery holiday but Chris loved it and so did I and afterwards I was very complimented that he enjoyed travelling with me.

So we will be off again as soon as we can afford it! I feel very refreshed after the holiday. Even three days helps put things into perspective a little and the fresh air and mild climate were great. Also practising Italian and seeing all the new sights and sounds is great for stimulating the brain which had got a bit sluggish. Chris is great to travel with and I couldn't have done it without him. He cut quite a dash too - the true Englishman abroad

Thursday March 22, 2007 - 07:16pm

Life goes on

Well the window has been repaired and there has been no further trouble. I have put Andy out of my mind and my life now I know what he is capable of, and Chris and I are getting on better than ever. We went out for an Indian meal last weekend which was excellent service but average food and crazy lighting which made the menu totally illegible and turned the food pink :)

Yesterday was Mother's day. On Saturday we drove down to Suffolk to the farm to pick up my daughter's Dyson Hoover, that she wants us to post to Ireland, and toured round all my old haunts which was great. When we got back there were two boxes of flowers from her waiting on the doorstep. I love flowers and have been enjoying them today.

My parents are back from Goa reasonably safely though a day late, which set us all worrying, but they are as cheerful as ever. They played a lot of golf out there. (They are in their mid eighties ...I mean age not temperature!)

Ann Lawson

Saturday April 7, 2007 - 07:42pm

Medication and all I hate about it

Antipsychotics are beloved of doctors and mostly hated by patients and public. There are two main sorts; typical and atypical. The older sorts (typical) are the ones I am on (piportal palminate) are likely to cause weight gain and a high level of extra pyramidal effects that is side effects. The chief amongst these is Tardive dyskinesia which is an uncontrollable movement disorder which psychiatrist like Peter Breggin in the states has successful negotiated massive compensation claims for. The new generation of drugs, atypical, cause even greater weight gain and often diabetes. I am on one of the strongest typical antipsychotics but do not wish to chance my luck moving to an atypical one, as the benefits, if any seem very marginal and the disadvantages even greater in the long term. They are better tolerated but I want to get off antipsychotics altogether.

My diagnosis is bipolar, not that I pay much attention to that as everyone I know is bipolar and it's just a convenient tag to hang a treatment regime on someone. However my drug regime is basically no different from when I was diagnosed schizophrenic. They know, damn well, I wouldn't take the antipsychotics unless they were forced on me so I have to attend the community psychiatric nurse once a fortnight for a slow release injection in the buttock. There is a tiny marginal reduction in amount every 3 months.

And how does this affect my life? Well, I have twice been diagnosed with Tardive dyskinesia by psychiatrists and the immediate action recommended for this is suspension of antipsychotics. Has this happened? No! I rock backwards and forwards all day long and can't sit still. At night I have restless legs and my feet move 19 to the dozen. The antipsychotics reduce the amount of dopamine transmitted in the brain. Dopamine is a chemical transmitter. In cases of Parkinson disease dopamine agonists are used to increase the amount of dopamine in the brain to prevent the movement disorders that are a symptom of Parkinson's. Antipsychotics induce a side effect spectrum that imitates Parkinson's. When you smoke a cigarette dopamine is boosted in the brain. The majority of mental patients smoke probably just to counter the awful effect of antipsychotics, which is another very good reason to discontinue them. If it were known that psychiatric drugs were causing patients to smoke more then there would be an outcry, which is why they keep quiet about that particular effect.

I remember when I was last off antipsychotics about two years ago. I could sit without constant restlessness and movement and concentrate and relax, I really felt normal. It was a few months to reach that stage and all I got off the doctors during that time was 'do you want your injection?' In the end because I refused my injection they took away my driving license and sectioned me. You cannot legally refuse medication when you are sectioned in hospital. The new mental health bill that is coming out includes community treatment orders by which you will be legally bound to take your medication in the community not just when you are sectioned.

And finally weight. God, yes, weight! When I last came off my antipsychotics I was losing a 1lb a week without trying and able to eat good healthy meals. Now I am consistently gaining weight whatever I do. I am obese and struggle daily with my weight. I have digital scales and use them numerous times a day only to see no change in the dial except upwards. It's so disheartening. I am even on a slimming pill now, prescribed by my doctor, but there is still no change except upwards. I am 13stone 5lbs and sick to death of the struggle.

My concentration is also poor. Last time I was off antipsychotics I did an online Oxford University course and gained 10 credits; the maximum. When I tried to do another on the drug I couldn't even get started.

So what are the advantages of antipsychotics? Well I sleep a lot (day and night) when restless legs don't wake me up. I don't think so much and I am less irritable. The only significant advantage personally I experience is that the doctors and nurses are over the moon when I comply with medication and shit scared when I don't. What other illness is there where you cannot legally refuse medication? Apparently there are some age old tuberculosis laws that still insist on medication compliance. But even if you have cancer you can decide to die rather than receive treatment.

So here we have a very strong medication administered by a non negotiable injection (they don't trust me to take pills) Which causes massive weight gain, uncontrollable movement disorders, which are often permanent, and increases your desire to smoke. Is this progress? Is it civilised to insist millions of people take this? And why are doctors so blind to the uselessness of these drugs. Perhaps it's all the freebies they get from the drug companies. Soon it will be enshrined in law that I must be permanently disabled by these drugs and I think it's a total civil liberty issue. I really don't know where I go from here.

Entry for April 13, 2007

Yes I was a bit upset the other night after not sleeping but I put a lid on it as soon as I talked to Chris and we had a great Easter here in Norwich and also in North Norfolk where he lives. This weekend he has his son David staying so I went up the local pub on my own tonight at 10 and there was music on. I had a good natter and laugh with my old buddies and an excellent little dance. It was lovely to see my security light in action on the house when I returned and it really is pretty. I might Hoover up and mow the lawn tomorrow after Chris has called. He is borrowing the car for a day to take David round. Then they are both coming over Sunday. My daughter's Hoover still hasn't arrived in Ireland. We sent it the week before Easter. But she says not to worry and she is in excellent form. Apparently the weather is brilliant and she is getting sun burnt (April!). It has turned misty here for the last couple of days so I haven't been able to sunbathe in my new chair. Let's hope it isn't too hot in June- July with this global warming. We have booked flights to Ireland for late June so that should be fun.

Well I have neglected my blog for a while. I have been very busy what with my birthday and my parent's birthday. I have bought an electric piano too and have been having fun playing that whenever I have a spare moment. We had brilliant weather in April but May has been a bit of a washout. Chris and I went to Bedfordshire to a model aeroplane day last Sunday at Shuttleworth, but it must have been the wettest day of the year and I sat outside in my fisherman's chair to get a good view and it was even too wet to light a cigarette. It was fascinating going round the hangers seeing all the full sized old planes they have in the hangers there. Some days they actually fly them. Chris loved it so I guess we will be going again. The journey wasn't too bad at all and my little car made it easily.

I am doing some work as a service user down the hospital now. We are 'experts by experience' and the authorities are falling over themselves to get our views...especially if they are positive. We get paid expenses too which is very nice and a massive improvement on my last job. If the hospital trust becomes a foundation hospital, I have been asked to apply as a service user governor.

I have to see my shrink today for a meeting, mainly to discuss medication and Chris is meeting me there. As I had that blip when I ran out of sleeping pills recently, I am worried he won't reduce my injection a bit more. They are so bloody cautious.

There is a service user party this weekend we may well go to, and on Sunday Mum and Dad want us to go down to Suffolk for a walk.

The garden has looked lovely this spring, but it is beginning to fade now and I noticed yesterday that it needs another good weed. With all this rain the grass is getting long again too

Birthday

I had a splendiferous birthday with loads of flowers and a barbecue.

Thursday April 26, 2007 - 12:23am

Seven years continual recovery after 30 years of mental illness
Cognitive Behavioural Therapy (CBT)

This is recommended; by everyone I know both professionals and patients as a way to overcome mental illness, depression, anxiety and other problems without drugs.

Saturday June 16, 2007 - 09:13am

Ann Lawson

Smoking ban

Now only 2 weeks until we will not be able to relax in
any public enclosed space. Interestingly there
have been a few emails from smokers in Wales, Scotland, and
Ireland
who already have bans in place, saying they have met new friends,
girl/ boyfriends, and even one wife thanks to the ban, and the
social nature of popping outside from the pub for a smoke. Just
a glimmer of hope for those of you dreading 1/7.

Saturday June 16, 2007 - 12:11am

The Weekend

Chris and I met up at a smart restaurant on the prettiest medieval
street in Norwich yesterday with three of my girlfriends and we had
a lovely al fresco lunch with beer. When things like that happen it is
great to get over your nerves and really enjoy it, then you feel you
have achieved something. In the evening I cooked a fabulous meal
which I pinched off the celebrity chef programme the night before
on telly, (one of the very few times I watch telly). Then we went to
the pub. Yesterday it was warm but the sun didn't really shine; yet
for some reason everyone had a smile on their face and a cheery
hello. I really feel I am making friends now instead of just sitting,
sulking and depressed as I used to when I was ill.

This morning I wasn't too pleased with what the weighing scales
told me but it is another mild day and I am just about to go out and
listen to the birds in my sunbathing chair with a fag before I get up.
Chris is still asleep. There is a band playing in the park today so we
are going to that and we are also going to see the model boats and
trains that run there on a Sunday.

Life is good and I am happy. We are off to Ireland in two weeks to
see my daughter!!!!!!

Thursday June 28, 2007 - 09:15am

Ireland

Well Chris and I are off to Ireland tomorrow to stay with my daughter, Tanya and her boyfriend Reinier, a Dutchman she met in South Africa. They live in County Mayo, Newport, which is right on the West Coast. Reinier has just broken his ankle so I expect it will be a busy holiday, helping walk the two dogs, cook, clean and shop. We are flying with Ryan air where they squeeze people in so I am not looking forward to the flight! We are taking the bus to Stansted then we have a hire car waiting at the other end. Of course there is a no smoking policy in Ireland now so that will be tricky too. The ban over here starts July 1st so it will be good practice. Today I have to pack and I will take my new camera and if I can work out how to use it, should come back with some good photos to post on here. I am nervous as hell! Chris is really looking forward to it. We will be back on Monday. Au revoir!

Friday July 13, 2007 - 11:54pm

Visit to My Daughter in Ireland

Well we had a terrific time in Ireland, Chris and I, staying with my daughter Tanya and her Dutch boyfriend Reinier who has just broken his ankle. Tanya was blooming and has lost loads of weight. They have a lovely house they rent in Newport, which is a pretty coastal town on the West Coast. They are looking at a rural house they hope to buy and do up. They have two dogs, one a noisy Jack Russell and one a silent Japanese dog that will grow to the size of a small donkey. They walk them twice a day on the beach.

Both of them are working, though Tanya is a little disappointed she can't use her teaching qualifications there because she doesn't know Irish and with her being dyslexic she doesn't think she can learn it. I haven't spent time with Tanya for years, so it was just lovely to catch up and get to know Reinier a little. I told her, she will have to invite her father who now lives in America to stay. She hasn't seen him since she was 3, although they are in touch by e-mail.

I liked Ireland. Of course the mountains are wonderful after flat East Anglia but the people, though not effusive, are funny and helpful. There was a great 'craic' in the pubs and shops and cafes (that means atmosphere) and it was interesting to get a taste of the smoking ban before it comes in here. I took everyone out for two meals, but Tanya is a brilliant cook and hostess. The supermarkets were stocked high with really mouth-watering food. I think we will be going again regularly especially as there is an international airport at Knock, right close to her and the flights are so cheap on Ryan Air. I brought back a small plastic bottle of holy water from Knock so I should be all right now! ;)

Friday June 1, 2007 - 01:09am

Rain, rain, rain and not a drop to drink!

I am doing a cognitive behaviour therapy course on the net and the last module was on challenging unhelpful thinking. I wasn't completely convinced by it and in fact have launched on a whole new theory of world politics which perhaps you can help me challenge! I have trouble with the hereafter...that is I'll be going to do something and then completely forget to do it as I get side-tracked. For example I'll go into the bedroom and forget what I'm hereafter. Now is this just old age or is it, as so many people suffer from it, a sign that the world lacks leadership and we are not sure where we are going hereafter. For example what is the endgame in Iraq?

It's just a thought (and probably a crazy one at that!)

Only You Can Cure Yourself

This painting is a portrait of a member of the de Broglie family painted by Ingres in the 19th century. That is the family I stayed with when I first became confused; I had no idea they were anything but strangers and it was a job when in fact members of their family had stayed on our farm and lived with us as kids.

Thursday August 9, 2007 - 03:25pm

Gall Stones

Chris had an operation at long last on his gall stones last Tuesday so I donned my nurses uniform (with the short skirt) and looked after him for a couple of days then his son David came down from London and took over till yesterday. I'm going out to Holt today to see how he is and probably we will go to the seaside. I'm sorry I haven't a gory photo of his keyhole surgery and bruising ;)

As you all know the UK has been under a few feet of water. In fact it has been wet here since May. We are planning a barbecue for a few friends, but are just having to wait, until we can be sure there won't be a downpour.

The smoking ban is in place and I have only heard of one death; a bouncer who told someone to stop smoking and was shot.

Ann Lawson

Entry for October 15, 2007

I had another great weekend. All the tension just flowed out of me as I got out of Norwich. We walked on the beach and had lunch at a small café, then went to see the steam trains and had a ride on the miniature railway. The weather on Saturday was particularly sunny.

This Monday morning though I am thinking back to the character assassination my community nurse wrote and made me sign at our last meeting...full of inaccuracies and dredging up things from 1978. They are so stupid. They give you no encouragement and totally fail to understand me. The mental health authorities are crap. It is all about social control and I wouldn't be surprised if they are actually keen to make people kill themselves with the shit that they throw at you and expect you to keep smiling on. Still I only have to see her once a month now and his Excellency the shrink once every six months. So I have a bit of time before the next character assassination to gather my confidence and happiness. All the time I have to take their fucking drugs, which make me fat and slothful. My advice to you is; never ever get involved with the mental health services. If you decide you don't want them anymore they will go out of their way to have you hospitalised and brought back in line. As everyone knows if you are not mad when you go into hospital you sure will be when you come out. There are hardly any solicitors who will act for you either. So even though life is comfortable for me whenever I make an attempt to branch out and work the 'effing' authorities panic. I mean if I want to use my brain and get some where in life they are certain to stamp on it. Free country? Rubbish!

Monday October 15, 2007 - 01:35am

Difficult Week

This has been a bit of a difficult week for me. Chris's son started university, which was stressful for Chris but a terrific achievement for his son who has Asperger's syndrome, which is a mild form of autism. I would recommend reading 'the curious incident of the dog in the night' if you want to know more about Asperger's. I've just finished it.

Only You Can Cure Yourself

Then I had to get to know a new psychiatrist and was sure he was going to be an unintelligible foreigner, but he turned out to be a dapper and literate Nigerian who was very charming. I didn't get my medication reduction but at least I only have to have injections once a month now instead of every two weeks. Also I only have to see him every six months instead of every three. So there is some progress. Chris came with me. I'm not sure I would have been as self-controlled as I was if he hadn't. I was getting very worked up about the meeting.

Finally I have a new companion in the house and this was the most stressful thing for me. He is a 23 - year - old polish economic migrant and it has taken some time to negotiate a modus Vivendi. I was worried it was affecting Chris and my relationship and also worried about my own safety with a stranger from the Internet lodging in the house. Just before meeting the psychiatrist it all came to a head and there was a little shouting on my part when I told him he had three weeks to leave. He kept to himself for a couple of days after that and things settled down and now I feel happier about the whole thing. I am hoping it was just all the stress built up together that caused me to get angry. I don't really mind now if he goes or stays but at least there is no bad feelings any more and Chris as usual has been very cool about it, although I think he has felt the tension.

Then there has been some good news as my daughter has invited Chris and me to stay at her house in Ireland for Christmas. I am not sure yet if we will go but it could be a nice holiday for a few days and I very much want a holiday.

And finally there is some sad news about my niece who wouldn't go to school and my brother put her in an adolescent psychiatric unit, which made me very cross with him. Now she is back and very, very ill and suicidal. So I am steering clear of a family, with such a penchant for psychiatry, like mine. I think mental illness is a direct result from the treatment, I think that it is best if possible to leave it well alone. All the 35 year's of treatment certainly never helped me and in the end I had to ask myself "why do I keep on going back to hospital?" and with a lot of struggle and a bit of help from my daughter we came up with a realistic answer. It is very difficult to escape the clutches of psychiatry, but since then I have been making good progress in my life. I wasn't before. I think, perhaps, the authorities are beginning to recognise this although they cannot understand my explanation of why it has happened. It is all very tedious dealing with them. I repeat myself over and over again but they simply don't understand.

So I'm sorry if I haven't chatted to friends much on here recently and sorry if I have been a bit short, profane and worked up but I hope that now things will settle down a bit. I would still like a holiday but I may have to go on my own as Chris hasn't the finance and he doggedly refuses to allow me to pay. I'm sure now his son is settling well in university we will work something out soon. Best wishes to everyone.

Friday October 5, 2007 - 01:19pm

Beautiful Autumn

I am very lucky because I live in the city but Chris lives in the country so we visit each other and both get the best of both worlds. The weekend before last I even swam in the sea. It is the first time the weather has been good enough this year and the sea warm enough.

This weekend I stayed with Chris again and on Saturday we went to Cromer and walked about the town then visited a cafe on the sea front where we sat outside. On Sunday we went on a lovely walk collecting sloes and crab apples because Chris wants to make sloe gin and crab apple jelly as Christmas presents. Then we dropped in at a pub for a bite to eat further up the coast.

The weather this September has been lovely and today (Sunday) was sunny with a balmy wind and really quite warm. It's a real joy after months and months of rain. The last time we could enjoy the outdoors was April.

Barbecue

Well my girl friends persuaded me to do a barbecue on bank holiday Monday, giving me a day and a half warning. We had been planning one for months and that seemed like the first fine day. So I invited about 30 (!) people and tidied the garden (!) and set about the shopping and planning. The barbecue went very well indeed, with Chris doing an excellent job as chef, it seemed to be enjoyed by all. Most people behaved very well but one of my drunken friends from my past life did get a bit out of order at the end and we had a job getting him home. Yesterday I was shattered all day. It must have been the quiet after the storm as I was useless all day. My age and the drugs don't help but I'm only just beginning to feel human again today. Still it was great fun. People brought so much food themselves that I packed up doggy bags for some of the guests to take home, which were much appreciated.

I'll take it easy again, today, as I still feel a little blasted. But my good humour is coming back. Yesterday my head was just swimming all day :)

On Sunday Chris and I are going to an air-show at Old Warden, Shuttleworth College, Bedfordshire. Dad, who was a pilot in the war is going too and meeting a mate of his from the war there. So we are hoping to meet up for a picnic and watch the vintage planes take off. It should be a great day although the weather forecast isn't brilliant.

Sunday September 23, 2007 - 01:51pm

Good Weekend

Well at long last I have seen Chris's planes fly. We went to Old Warden at Biggleswade and the weather was actually fine. It is just over a two hour drive (Chris drives my car) and Chris's favourite place. He loaded all his planes, and bits and pieces to mend them, into my little car and off we went with our coffee flasks and sandwiches. As we had been the weekend before to an air-show of full size planes and met Dad and his old solicitor there who had both been Second World War pilots, I wasn't that keen to go again. But in fact it was magical. All these little planes were buzzing about: noisy ones, quiet ones and the men totally absorbed in their hobbies; Very few women. Some of the planes, made of tissue paper and balsa wood were as beautiful as dragon flies or fairies. And Chris's really flew well. So well in fact that one flew right away and we couldn't find it.

It was a great atmosphere and I got chatting to a lot of these strange old boys. As Chris says at least when they are chasing planes their wives know they are not chasing women!

Sunday July 29, 2007 - 12:53am

Bad Weather And Celebrations

Conversation in the UK traditionally was about the weather. With global warming we have even more to talk about now. Not only is the weather uncertain from day to day as before; now it is extreme too. We have had wet weather for three months now and many homes have been so severely flooded out the government has given money for assistance; so far £8 million. The gardens are growing like the day of the triffids and I have been planning a barbecue for my close friends for weeks but there just hasn't been a suitable weather slot. Last year we had a heat wave in July so it seems nothing is certain any more and its all rather science fiction. Of course we aren't alone and stories come in from all over the world of unusual and extreme weather conditions. Strangely there are still many odd bods who don't believe that the weather is unusual and global warming is with us.

Today is the Lord Mayor's parade here in Norwich and there are celebrations all day. Chris wants to see it all, as he is new to it so we are going to join the throngs. Also a girl friend of mine has a fiftieth birthday party in the city tonight so we shall drop in on that too if it's not crowded out. The forecast? Well naturally it's for rain! :)

Sunday November 11, 2007 - 09:04am

Entry for October 23, 2007

The Critical Psychiatry website

I would recommend this website to anyone who has suffered from mental illness and wants a broader perspective.

Family Life

This film by Ken Loach (along with a lot of anti-psychiatry books) radically influenced my view of mental illness when I was at university before I was ever caught in the system.

It is a tragic irony that some one like me so opposed to psychiatry should have been treated so severely by the mental health authorities and family for over three decades, whereas people who ask for help are unlikely to get any.

Tuesday October 23, 2007 - 04:12pm

We Are Going To Ireland!

Well I was up at 2.00 this morning writing a brilliant blog and when I went to save it, it disappeared, :(so you will only get a very much shortened version now.

We have booked our tickets for Ireland for Christmas. Hell of a trek for one day but should be fun. Another great weekend last weekend - picnicking and gathering sloes in the brilliant sunshine. I have been Feeling more cheerful. Sorry about the last depressing blog. Even found some lipstick I have been missing for two years this morning! Arranged a deposit for my daughter and Reinier to buy a house but don't want to rush them. Polish lodger settling in well. Chris is coming over tomorrow. We are meeting Mum and Dad for a meal in Southwold next week.

My tip to everyone "take a holiday; it may be a long winter"
Tuesday October 16, 2007 - 07:39pm

October is mental health month

Life is too short for drama & petty things!
So laugh insanely, love truly and forgive quickly!

From one unstable person to another
Hope everyone is happy in their head - we're all doing' pretty good
in mine!

Friday November 23, 2007 - 01:50pm

Countdown to Christmas

My dear old Mum came to visit yesterday and it has really cheered
me up. Both Chris and I have been quite depressed, in fact I have
been taking St John's Wort, as I can't afford a S.A.D. light. But
seeing Mum has made me feel loads better. Makes me wonder how
I will cope when she is gone for good. I'll probably turn into a
grumpy old woman, :) which isn't far from the truth now.

I'm pretty well organised for Christmas, just got to buy the lodger's
present and my daughter's boyfriend's. Soon I will have to settle
down to writing cards and begin to get ready for our couple of days
in Ireland with Tanya. I am preparing a stocking for her (she is 25!)
and have bought loads of little odds and ends, some cheap, some
expensive. We have to be careful on the weight limit for the flight
and I'm not sure how much liquid we can take.

The saga of the New Zealand branch of the family continues. My
sister has bought another house, which does look very nice.
Meantime her ex partner has found a new girlfriend on the net in
Thailand. Then their daughter threw a wobbly when she found out
so now Peter is reassessing his future. They are in the middle of
selling the family home.

The lodger is well settled in and no trouble. In fact I think he is
terrified of me, :) He came in at 12.30 last night from work and sat
down here on the computer till 3.00. Then Chris decided he wanted
a 'cuppa', so Chris and I had two 'cuppas' in bed and a great chat as
we always do in the middle of the night. Now both Chris and the
lodger are asleep but I can't sleep any more so I came down here to
write my blog.

I have the feeling "my cup runneth over" I am so comforted and
warm and happy. When I think back to all those years of pain and

guilt and misery I had when I was ill I just cannot believe how lucky I am now, with my family and friends.

Chris and I watched "the meaning of life" by Monte Python last night, which I happened to have on my shelves and that was fun. Then we went for a walk in the park in the dark.

I must watch my weight. Both Chris and I are creeping up. Mum looked so well and slim.

Anyway I hope those who read this are managing to banish the winter blues and looking forward to a happy Christmas. Annie

Wednesday November 21, 2007 - 10:59pm

Poem

Things that go 'bump' in the night,

should really not give you a fright,

it's the hole in the ear,

that lets in the fear,

that, and the absence of light.

Spike Milligan

Saturday December 29, 2007 - 11:26pm

Chris, Tanya and Reinier; Ireland Christmas day 2007

Tanya and Reinier treated us royally. They are very uncertain as to their plans but Tanya seemed to cheer up by the time we had left. Chris and I had a tiff when we got home but it didn't last long.

Ann Lawson

Run up to New Year

Well Chris and I are having a tiff since getting back from Ireland. I won't see him till New Year's Eve as he has gone to London.

Meantime I am quite busy with work demands but suffering from an unpleasant cold.

I have the glad eye a bit whilst this tiff goes on. Cruel of me I know but the aftermath to Christmas is always difficult.

We are hoping to gather at the local for New Year's Eve. There are new licensees and some improvements have been made. On the other hand the local shop has closed and not reopened yet.

I think it is very true we all need closeness; it softens the edges.

With best Wishes to one and all for New Year's Eve.

Only You Can Cure Yourself

Entry for December 19, 2007

Merry Crimble!

Tuesday December 18, 2007 - 07:58am

Chaos and Disorder

Well the ranks are disunited and the leadership is at sea. Firstly the
mental health authorities, who I have to see every month
WITHOUT FAIL OR THE HEAVENS WILL DESCEND to have
an injection up the arse, buggered me about so I had to miss a great
afternoon coppicing with the friends of Eaton Park of which I am
vice chair. Then, incredulously, I phoned up DVLA to see how my
driving licence renewal application was going, which I had done all
the work for including filling in the form and seeing my new
consultant with it over two months ago, and found out that they
wrote to some other top consultant, whose name they said I had
given them (I never even knew he existed till 2 days ago) on the 1st
of November and again on the 29th of November to remind him to
return another form before the renewal is confirmed. Some other
arsehole consultant several years ago when I was under section had
forced me to write to DVLA to say I was bipolar (which I don't
think I am) so now I have to renew my license every year. As there
have been no problems this year and I am on a low dose of
medication taken regularly I presumed this would be automatic. But
because the authorities don't know there arses from their elbows, I
am now going to be without a driving license YET AGAIN over
Christmas and if I lose my cool probably all year again.

Total Page Views
5,878

Row, row, row your boat, gently down the stream. Merrily, merrily,
merrily, merrily, life is but a dream

Ann Lawson

Troubled Times

Things have not been good since coming back from Ireland. My daughter has been badly shaken at losing her job. She wants to leave Ireland and resettle in New Zealand. For the meantime we have agreed she goes on Holiday there and visits my sister and her daughter and also she has decided to visit all the family in England in February. I think that is a good plan and hope it restores her confidence and enables her to see things more clearly. If it doesn't she may need some counselling again. Her boyfriend Reinier is standing by her. I have had some more wallet surgery!

When I got back from Ireland I was infected by Tanya's cut and run theory and virtually chucked Chris. It was only seeing my dearest friend Sarah with him last weekend that brought me to my senses. But it will take a long time to repair the damage. I have been horrid to him.

Anyway Tanya hopefully is dropping by for lunch on the 20th February and I am looking at my cookbooks to give her a real treat. Also I have booked a week's holiday in Tenerife, something I have needed for a long time, but couldn't persuade Chris to come with me, so I am going alone.

My main worry is Tanya. As Reinier agrees it would be lovely to see her happy again but it may take some time. No way would I ever want her to go down the path of mental health that I did but she needs some rest and recuperation. She was screaming down the phone at me the other day. I have made it quite clear to her that this is the last time I can bail her out financially. I think she should learn to take things easier like her poor old Mum does.

Chris will remain a good friend I think but whether we become lovers again I don't know.

I am quite calm and equitable now, but am worried when Tanya comes on the 20th, I may get upset again.

With her chequered child hood it is not surprising she is finding life difficult. I spoilt her rotten because I felt so guilty that I was ill and couldn't be a good mother and I think the rest of the family did too.

Also because she was so often in foster care and even full care she lacked continuity and, as she says, felt like a parcel being handed round. She has done very well, considering, and hopefully she will soon be back on her feet. Although I realise she may have other breakdowns. That is partly why I don't want her to move to New Zealand. Although she has family there it is too ambitious a move. Anyway mothers aren't always right.

Wednesday January 30, 2008 - 11:41pm

Unbelievably Christmas didn't end for us till this Sunday

Dad phoned a couple of weeks ago to arrange to meet us at Walberswick on Epiphany Sunday, as we hadn't seen them all over Christmas. Then Mum noticed some strange alternative booking they had for that day so Dad very sheepishly phoned back to rearrange for last Sunday, 13th January. So Chris and I drove down there (it's on Suffolk on the coast; very beautiful) and arrived ages early. There was a cold wind so we went to the Bell and had a coffee by the wood fire. Then we walked up to the Anchor with our prezzies for them. We both ordered a drink and sat down in the bar and looked at the reading matter lying about. Dad and Mum didn't arrive till the last moment and the staff hardly gave me time to say hello to them literally before they were herding us into the dining room. All I got was a 2-inch cheese soufflé and Dad had bought me a half. So I had to fill up on water and when Mum's barbed comments got too much I just walked out. I waited for Chris a bit then walked down to where I had stayed (the year after I first got ill) in a caravan with a couple of old friends of mine, I am still in touch with them. I went back to the Anchor to see if Chris was still there and he had left so I thanked them for the soufflé and walked back to the car. I sat on a boat trailer to make sure Chris could see me. He waved at me a moment later and he drove home, picking up his cigarettes I had left outside the Anchor on the way back. We stopped to have a thermos of coffee in the car at Blythburgh on the way back as I had missed my coffee at the Anchor, with all the upset, and to collect our senses.

When we got back Chris had a queasy tummy, so happily he stayed the night and the following morning I was pretty low so he stayed around for me for a bit. Mum and Dad phoned to thank us for the prezzies (flowers, sloe gin we had made and crab apple jelly we had made, but not the photograph of us in Ireland). They were both as high as kites. I even had another message on my answer phone this morning thanking us.

So Christmas is finally over and I have been doing some much needed financial housekeeping today.

I haven't heard from the job I applied for but with a family like mine I really don't know if I could possibly do a job, not that it looks like they are even inviting me for interview. I was complaining to Chris on Monday that life is boring. However I am involved in quite a few things with Hellesden Hospital and Eaton Park and neighbourhood committees, so I guess I am busy enough.

It has not been a bad Christmas. I was a bit upset Chris didn't see the funny side but then he hasn't had as much of an experience of them as I have! Mum keeps her daft sense of humour despite being totally bonkers.

Anyway that's another Christmas over and there were no deaths except the mother of a Jewish friend of mine and she was already in a home. I kept it together, just about, although at one point I thought I was pregnant! There were a few conjugal tiffs here and amongst my friends, but it was just lovely seeing my brother's family and visiting Tanya. She treated us so well. There was a touch of tactlessness on my part but I managed to apologise. I really liked the way she laughed at some of my bad jokes. Chris lost it a bit coming home but I think we'll manage to pick up the pieces. New Year's Eve was a dead loss. I do think Chris creates problems where there aren't any sometimes.

Anyway my three- year driving license has come through and my medication is very low even though I still have to attend for an injection every month.

God do you pay for family problems! Chris asked me what advice I would give to anyone to prevent what happened to me happening to them. I said 'more haste less speed.' Either that or don't have a mad mother.

Now Tanya has received a lot of money from me so the next journey in the Lawson family saga is what are Reinier and her going to do with it? I dread to think!

Hope your family isn't as screwed up as mine.

Tuesday January 15, 2008 - 09:10am

Lovely sunny day today

Saturday January 12, 2008 - 05:53am

January

January is a very difficult month for me as my brother killed himself this month. I know it was 1975 but it was an awful time. I had just been put in a mental hospital for the first time and discharged myself after a week and then Mum and dad and my two brothers came round to the flat in Norwich where I was sharing to say Roger was dead.

I made a cup of tea and then I forget.

After the funeral, which Mum and Dad's GP forbade me to go to; my sister drove me back to the mental hospital. I stayed there four months and could only get out by agreeing to work in a council old people's home as a bum wiper.

When I eventually got the sack, much to my relief, the psychiatrist said I had to live with my parents and leave the flat.

That was only the beginning of my troubles.

Thursday February 14, 2008 - 12:21pm

Tenerife holiday

Well I'm off to Tenerife on the 12th. I have pleaded with Chris to come on holiday with me since September, and before, but he wouldn't budge, till I was so low and bad tempered that with a bit of prompting from one of my 360 friends (thanks Chris Fleuty) I have booked a late deal holiday to Porto Cruz and am going on my own. I am flying from Norwich and all transfers are taken care of so it should be really easy. The weather is not sun scorching this time of year but I hope to read and walk and explore and perhaps swim. I hope to come back much refreshed and ready for the fray again. I have been working very hard at stuff for ages now and I think we all need a holiday as often as possible to maintain our sanity. Hopefully things will be back to normal when I get back. Even just planning it has given me a break from my worries. Then my daughter is dropping in for lunch the day after I get back. Chris is meeting me at the airport too. He really is a sweetie.

Wednesday February 20, 2008 - 01:14am

Written in Tenerife

It is really lovely to get some winter sun. I have been spending my time walking and swimming and writing postcards. Sitting in cafes drinking coffee and watching the world go by. North Tenerife gets quite a lot of rain so it is pretty green and very beautiful. The beaches are all volcanic black sand and the Atlantic rollers break on the rocks, but the sea is quite cold. I feel so spoilt staying here in this comfortable hotel with all my meals cooked and my bedroom cleaned everyday. I spend a lot of time around the town, but the pool here is the warmest to swim in.

It is easy to get a tan despite the cloudier weather in the north. There are a lot of oldies here and Germans. Every one understands English though and anyway you only need to shout a bit louder when you meet foreigners ;)

Only You Can Cure Yourself

Well I'm back from Tenerife!

I'm just beginning to acclimatise myself again to the English weather. I shoved the heating on full when I got home and haven't felt good for a couple of days...a bit of an upset tummy (yes I did drink the water!).

Chris met me at the airport I think more to see the planes than me but it was lovely to see him again although we had kept in touch throughout the holiday. He had felt a bit ropey when I had been away too. Anyway the following day my darling daughter dropped by and we went for a walk in the park, a coffee in the local and lunch at home. She had written her car off on the motorway so wasn't too happy!

Now it turns out Chris has sickness and diarrhoea too and is quite poorly.

I feel much happier after the holiday and can't imagine why anyone would want to go to a horrible hospital when they feel down, when with a bit of organisation you can go on holiday and come back feeling full of beans. I'll probably go out to Holt to see Chris this weekend, and take my new car for its first long run. It's a bit **ratterly** so it will be quite a test. Tanya my daughter is going to stay with her Granny and Granddad for a couple of days.

I'm a bit stuck for friends at the moment because my usual natterers, I am finding too ill to share things with willingly without upsetting them or them upsetting me. I need a few more energetic independent friends, who aren't hidebound by psychiatry, now I am leaving that scene behind. It sometimes happens that you out grow friends but I have known some of them for so many years it takes a while to find new friends for a girly natter. Also when I was on holiday I found looking back, my happiest times were when I was working so maybe I'll seriously look for some more work along with my normal committee commitments.

I have a meeting tonight with friends of Eaton Park which should be quite good but unfortunately my computer has lost the e mail with the minutes.

I still feel a little fragile, but I can't imagine how bad Chris must be feeling poor lad

Entry for March 08, 2008

Thinking of moving and buying a house

Not moving

I had a couple of looks at the house and decided not to move. The more I look at other places the more I realise how lucky I am to live here so I suppose it serves a purpose being tempted. The other house was just impracticable. I am so comfortable here and everything is easy to maintain and I have so much space. Don't all threaten to come and stay at once!

Saturday March 8, 2008 - 02:38pm

Mother's Day

Mother's day was good. Mum phoned just after I had had my bath. And Tanya phoned, but we had some communication difficulties and I really felt like putting the phone down but didn't as it was mother's day and ended up telling her to fuck off which isn't very nice. Unfortunately she has blocked my email address so I can't write to her and apologise. She is off to New Zealand soon to trek through North Island and visit my sister and her cousin in South Island. My friend Wal in New Zealand says the weather isn't too good today so I hope it isn't too bad for her trip; it's getting a bit late in the Summer there for a trip.

Sunday March 2, 2008 - 07:53pm

Sleep problems

My dad and Poor Chris suffered yesterday. I had spent two days cooped up in the house and had not been able to sleep. I was incandescent by last night but went to bed and took a sleeping pill and every thing else and feel better now. I get so depressed when I don't sleep.

Tuesday February 26, 2008 - 11:13pm

Me and my daughter

My daughter Tanya was born in 1982. I had been ill for 13 years by then. I left her father when I was 7 month's pregnant because he was violent and unfaithful. I was living in a homeless hostel. She was in and out of foster homes from a very early age. My father moved us from Felixstowe to Norwich to be nearer the family and my hospitalisations got even more severe and Tanya was always put in foster homes then. I had to fight tooth and nail to keep her out of care. However, when she was about 13 my father agreed that she should go into care. The social services even looked for a family to adopt her. All this had a devastating effect on both her and me. However she got to university and got a degree. Since my recovery in 2002, I have done everything in my powers to try and repair the relationship. It has been painstakingly slow and hard and expensive work. However I am beginning to see results. She has visited me twice this week and we got on well and for the first time in years we are beginning to relax and talk to each other. Chris has been a great help. I think Tanya may be just beginning to have a little confidence in me. It is very exciting.

Entry for April 23, 2008

You ask about sectioning Mimi: sectioning means that under a section of the Mental Health Act (i.e. a subdivision of the act) two doctors and a social worker (and usually several policemen) comes round to your house. They can break down your door and forcibly confine you to mental hospital to as many days or months that the section defines. E.g. the most common one I receive is section3, which means six months, and under it you can be forcibly medicated. There are voluntary patients in hospital but they are few and far between and would probably be sectioned anyway if they tried to leave. You can appeal with the help of a solicitor, whilst under section but there aren't that many mental health solicitors and appeals usually fail. I won my last one.

Wednesday April 23, 2008 - 07:50pm

Psychiatry without Drugs

Rufus May's film last night on television was about treating a junior doctor who was hearing voices and getting her back to work without drugs. Rufus himself suffered from schizophrenia when younger and by lying was accepted to train as a clinical psychologist and now works in the NHS. He is a major thorn in the side of the establishment, and one of the few bright encouraging sparks which gives some of us hope that our lives don't just have to be about taking mind numbing drugs, violent sectioning and forced medication, and then you have the intolerable side effects of some medications.

Only You Can Cure Yourself

Tuesday April 22, 2008 - 05:00pm

Washing on the line

A POEM

A clothes line was a news forecast
To neighbours passing by.
There were no secrets you could keep
When clothes were hung to dry.

It also was a friendly link
For neighbours always knew
If company had stopped on by
To spend a night or two.

For then you'd see the 'fancy sheets'
And towels upon the line;
You'd see the 'company table cloths'
With intricate design.

The line announced a baby's birth
To folks who lived inside
As brand new infant clothes were hung
So carefully with pride.

The ages of the children could
So readily be known
By watching how the sizes changed
You'd know how much they'd grown.
It also told when illness struck,
As extra sheets were hung;
Then nightclothes, and a bathrobe, too,
Haphazardly were strung

It said, 'Gone on holiday now'
When lines hung limp and bare.
It told, 'We're back!' When full lines sagged
With not an inch to spare.

Ann Lawson

New folks in town were scorned upon
If wash was dingy grey,
As neighbours carefully raised their
Brows, and looked the other way...

But clotheslines now are of the past
For dryers make work less.
Now what goes on inside a home
Is anybody's guess.

I really miss that way of life.
It was a friendly sign
When neighbours knew each other best
By what hung on the line! Anon.

Only You Can Cure Yourself

America

NEWS YOU WON'T FIND ON CNN

Happy Anniversary, America!
How Lethally Stupid Can One Country Be?
By David Michael Green: Watching George W. Bush in operation these last couple of weeks is like having an out-of-body experience. On acid. During a nightmare. In a different galaxy.

As he presides over the latest disaster of his administration, (No, it's not a terrorist attack - that was 2001! No, it's not a catastrophic war - that was 2003! No, it's not a drowning city - that was 2005! This one is an economic meltdown, ladies and gentlemen!) Bringing to it the same blithe disengagement with which he's attended the previous ones, you cannot but stop and gaze in stark, comedic awe, realising that the most powerful polity that ever existed on the planet twice picked this imbecilic buffoon as its leader, from among 300 million other choices. Seeing him clown with the Washington press corps yet once again - and seeing them fawn over him, laugh in all the right places, and give him a standing ovation, also yet once again - is the equivalent of having all your logic circuits blown simultaneously. Truly, the universe has a twisted and deeply ironic sense of humour.

David Michael Green is a professor of political science at Hofstra University in New York.

Tuesday March 25, 2008 - 12:06am

Easter

Well it looks like this Easter is a time for hibernation what with the weather and the traffic. I am going for a walk in the park as usual. Tomorrow and on Saturday I am meeting up with girlfriends and going to the Sainsbury Centre, which is an art centre at the university. So I shall brave the weather. Then Chris is coming over on Sunday.

I'm sorry about my last entry. I didn't know it had been published and would have deleted it long ago if I had. I was really quite depressed for a couple of days after my holiday, quite seriously so and worried my daughter. I suppose I should have confided in my community nurse but I didn't. I did try and make an appointment with the doctor but there were too many other people more ill for them to see me so I braved through it. Then I had some really bad news, our vegetable and baccy man who comes round in a van on Friday died after a street fight. It was headlines and everyone was upset. Some how, although it was very sad and I had a good weep, it brought me back to my senses and when Chris came over yesterday we had a lovely time. So now I will try and keep my activity levels up because that is why I was getting down and self absorbed. I was so used to doing nothing on holiday but swimming I started mouldering away here too and that is no good. You really have to make an effort to keep busy if you are going to be happy.

So may I wish everyone a very Happy Easter and excuse me or kick me if I ever start feeling sorry for myself again to the extent I was.

Weight Gain

I am so tired of putting on weight with these drugs (they call it medication). Being immobile makes it worse. The drugs just make me feel ill and I crave food all the time, especially carbohydrates. It is so disheartening checking the scales every morning and every night to find more weight piles on. I am in the very obese range which means; danger of cardiac incidents, stroke, diabetes and cancer. It is so boring constantly having to diet and yet still I'm putting weight on. I contacted the Norfolk advocacy project yesterday, because when the arseholes of mental health authorities finally get round to organising my CPA (next meeting with the shrink) next month, I hope they can represent me and I can push to get off these fucking drugs. Why should I spend my life feeling ill when it only serves the pompous stupid doctors worried about their massively paid jobs?

Only You Can Cure Yourself

Friday May 2, 2008 - 01:03am

1st May 2008

Today is a local election voting day and also May Day. I have a postal vote so voted some time ago. Last night I went to a home watch meeting in the local school. It was very good to get out of the house and see people. With my poor toe I am still a bit confined to the house because I don't enjoy walking on it. When I went for my injection, the day before, I had to walk to the market and get my baccy too, and with the pain of my toe, the bloody injection and community nurse, and the rain which I hadn't anticipated I sat down in the centre of the city and had a little weep. So yesterday I missed another meeting because I couldn't face going out when walking is so painful. The doctor has told me that it will take at least a month to heal.

After the meeting, Chris and I had our usual chat on the phone, and then I phoned my sister in New Zealand where she was just having her morning porridge. I just sounded out my daughter's plans as she is staying there at the moment (although typically she was still fast asleep). Ruth, my sister, and I had a good chat about things in general including the parents.

I was up in the night and polished off some important emails, so I have time this morning to add a bit to my blog. I do wish yahoo would put as much effort in maintaining 360 as we bloggers put into our blogs. It's pathetic.

Wednesday April 30, 2008 - 11:19pm

Entry for April 29, 2008
Watching paint dry

"You will have a roof over your head and regular meals." When had that never been the case? Never! So, why did this country doctor want me to be admitted to a mental hospital? I had a job to go to and a flat in Norwich. Ah Norwich! The end of the world. There is nothing beyond Norwich. But Norwich had one more treat for me: To be locked up with all the flotsam and jetsam, the lonely and angry, the pathetic and the condemned. Now I was one of the condemned. All because a religious backwoods doctor thought I should be. Normal for Norwich. n.f.n. That's what the medical doctors wrote on some patient's notes here in Norwich. And today 32 years later I must still attend the outreach clinic (for the chronically ill) to have an injection in the bum to quieten down my thought processes and make me fat and lazy. And what if I don't go? I will be locked up again. I know I've tried it several times. They will come with police and doctors and nurses and po-faced social workers. They will walk all over my privacy and home and take me away in handcuffs and throw me in the back of a van, the police laughing all the way till I am back on terra firma, the glorious asylum, for another few months. Either I must compromise my thought processes and accept that I am insane or get the 'treatment', regular meals and a roof over my head and repeated assault by the goon nurses until I accept the needle up my bum for the rest of my life.

Tuesday April 29, 2008 - 12:08am

Entry for April 25, 2008

My day hasn't been good. I meant to write the speech for the Lord Mayor today for when he comes to open our parks 80th birthday celebrations but I've put it off all day. Also I'm not enjoying my immobility. I really need to exercise. So I am planning to go for a good swim this weekend. I was going over to Chris's but I was worried about the driving so he has very kindly agreed to come over here again. I can't persuade him to swim but he will come with me. I must write that speech tomorrow.

Friday April 25, 2008 - 03:36pm

Entry for April 24, 2008

It's my birthday today (or yesterday if yahoo had their dates right!) I had a lovely day. Chris was terrifically generous and Mum and Dad and Dad's sister dropped by for tea. They are all in the eighties and put me to shame with how active they all are. I broke my toe the day before so am a bit immobile. I had to miss the friends of Eaton Park meeting last night as a result.

Thoughts for the day:

I don't suffer from insanity; I enjoy every minute of it.

I work hard because millions on welfare depend on me!

I used to have a handle on life, but it broke.

Don't take life too seriously; No one gets out alive.

You're just jealous because the voices only talk to me.

Beauty is in the eye of the beer holder.

Earth is the insane asylum for the universe.

I'm not a complete idiot. Some parts are missing.

Out of my mind. Back in five minutes.

God must love stupid people; He made so many.

The gene pool could use a little chlorine.

Consciousness: That annoying time between naps.

Ever stop to think, and forget to start again?

Being "over the hill" is much better than being under it!

Procrastinate Now!

I have a degree in liberal arts; do you want fries with that?

A hangover is the wrath of grapes.

A journey of a thousand miles begins with a cash advance.

Stupidity is not a handicap. Park elsewhere!

He who dies with the most toys is nonetheless dead.

A picture is worth a thousand words, but it uses up three thousand times the memory.

Ham and eggs. A day's work for a chicken, a lifetime commitment for a pig.

The original point and click interface was a Smith and Wesson.

Make your words sweet & tender today, for tomorrow you may have to eat them.

Thursday May 15, 2008 - 11:52am

Dreams
Dream Catcher

A woman in the forest holds a dream catcher which ensnares the flowing images of her dreams. Bad dreams are dissolved by the dew, while good dreams are woven into the fabric of this world by Spiderwoman. May we all filter out our negative imagery before it becomes real in this life. For all that is manifested on this plane was first a dream in someone's mind. May we aspire to dream dreams in harmony with the whole of life.

Wednesday May 14, 2008 - 06:30

Poem by W D Yeats

He wishes for the Cloths of Heaven

Had I the heavens' embroidered cloths,
Enwrought with golden and silver light,
The blue and the dim and the dark cloths of night and light and the half-light,

Only You Can Cure Yourself

I would spread the cloths under your feet:
But I, being poor, have only my dreams;
I have spread my dreams under your feet;
Tread softly because you tread upon my dreams.

Tuesday May 13, 2008 - 04:26pm

Summer is here

Smiles and summer frocks. It's the first time we have felt any real heat in the sun. I have been sitting outside pubs smoking and drinking real ale. Touring the open-air cafes up the city to meet friends and read and have a coffee or a cake. The garden has been growing rampant and it's still full of colour. I have my tomato plants to get in the tub and several bedding plants I have bought to brighten up the area round the back. The cat came to visit me again yesterday. She hasn't been round in months.

I had a lovely weekend away at Chris's. I am reading quite a lot at the moment, which is a great pleasure. Chris is reading Pepys diaries; he lived in the early 17th century. It's a fascinating peep at life then through his eyes. We are going to Old Warden in Essex to fly model planes next weekend. It is Chris's favourite place as he meets all his friends and other model planes enthusiasts. Chris designs and builds model aeroplanes.

News

Well my daughter is back from New Zealand and staying with my younger brother on the farm. She has managed to land a job in Essex teaching whilst she was still in New Zealand and is going to see the school on Monday. She looks very well and popped up to see me the day after she landed!

Chris worked last night on a one off night shift stocktaking books and is home now catching up on his sleep upstairs. He needs the money to hire a car to transport his son and clobber back home from University at the end of term.

I phoned an old friend in Bristol last night and told her of the two deaths; she knew both of them as she was at the same school. She now had the Internet at home and wanted my sister's e-mail so she can contact her in New Zealand. They were very good friends at school.

I am going to see my parents next weekend whilst Chris is up in London and I'm also going to have a meal with my brother and sister in law. We've planned to celebrate their and my birthday. Don't know who will pay!

The preparations for the 80th Birthday of the local park are growing apace. I have some leafleting to do sometime. The Lord Mayor is coming and two dragons and other dignitaries! It all happens on the 15th of June so you are all welcome!

Anyway I have a Sikh coming to decorate my kitchen this morning so I'll sign of.

 Pinch, punch for the first of the month. Flaming June

Sunday June 1, 2008 - 02:01am

Medication

I had an hour-long interview with some wimp of a psychiatrist the other day. She had never met me before but she concluded from a glance at my notes that in 10 years time if I stay out of hospital she might reduce my drugs by an eighth.

I was first admitted because I had an abortion privately rather than see a psychiatrist and go through the system in 1975. This crime!!!!! Meant I was admitted to hospital. Since then I have been at odds with the medical profession as I repeatedly refused to take my medication and would be admitted to hospital. Now they look at my repeated admissions and use it as a reason to insist I take my medication. It is unbelievable.

Anyway you can imagine how I have been celebrating knowing that in 80 years time I will be off medication.

Only You Can Cure Yourself

Tuesday May 27, 2008 - 09:19am

Tears of grief

I heard today of the deaths of two of the finest people; both wonderful school friends. One was the daughter of a psychiatrist and her sister Kate was in my class...a right little rebel and so kind. Lesley had vitality, kindness and a sense of humour and great sensitivity. She had been under the mental health authorities for years. She drowned herself in the sea when she was on respite there. Then I made a phone call I had been putting off to my friend Kathy who has had Hodgkinsons disease (cancer). She passed away peacefully this weekend. She was one of my closest and dearest friends; very bright and loving. A good socialist and a civil servant like her father. She went to Oxford University. I had drifted apart from both of them but was hoping to get closer again and now will never have a chance. Death is such an ending, blackness, such an end to communication. Bless them both for enriching my life and curse me for abandoning them when I was ill. The world is a poorer place without both of them.

God bless...apparently the trick is to work on the present and let the future take care of itself I heard on the radio today. Of course don't ruminate on the past, nostalgia is a comfortable zone to be in but bad memories are best forgotten.
Wednesday May 28, 2008 - 06:31pm

Diary

I had a great weekend out at Holt with Chris. We went for a walk in the local park, which was jammed full of wonderful flowering rhododendrons of all different colours and then had a nice lunch outside in Sheringham by the sea. I dropped by my friend Sarah's on the way home in an attempt to cheer her up. She is feeling a bit suicidal at the moment.

My daughter flies back from New Zealand on Wednesday. I am not sure what she will do then, but I am hoping that she goes back to Ireland with her boyfriend Reinier. She has been staying with my sister and there have been very good reports of her, which is nice for me.

Tomorrow I am going to my friend's funeral; she drowned herself in the sea. I hope Chris will come with me. I also have my jab up the arse, which I finally agreed to go back on without too much trauma. I am quite optimistic about coming off it eventually or at least having it reduced.

I am worried about my smoking. My chest is really bad and I cough, cough, and cough. I phoned up about some hypnotherapy today but unfortunately they don't do it Norwich.

My brother tells me that my sister is coming over from New Zealand for Christmas. I think Chris and I are planning a quiet Christmas this year after going to Ireland last year. But there are sure to be problems. Perhaps Tanya and Reinier will come over from Ireland, :)

I haven't heard from my New Zealand friend Wal for a very long time. I've tried phoning but can't get a number and I've emailed. As he is over 80, I fear the worst. I may send him a card snail mail when I have some stamps.

I'm walking better and feeling a little gayer in the happy sense. Not reading much but trying to get fitter and am not feeling depressed. However I have put on about 4lbs since my holiday in Tenerife. Chris has put some weight on too. Since his gall stone operation we don't have to be so careful on fat.

Ann Lawson

Thursday May 29, 2008 - 11:19pm

Death and the psychiatric establishment

Well I had a pretty frustrating day yesterday. Firstly I ended up having an hour's discussion about reducing my medication by less than an eighth with the top shrink and my community psychiatric nurse but was getting no where. They reckon the benefit of the medicine outweighs the cost. Personally I don't think any medication likely to cause stroke, heart attack and diabetes is worth the cost, and these are supposed to be medical people! The shrink said, perhaps if I had 10 years out of hospital instead of just two, then she might consider slightly reducing my medication. It took an hour to get even that concession from her, which naturally is useless because at the rate my weight is going up at the moment I will be well dead by then. She couldn't even do the basic mental arithmetic; I had to do it for her. What on earth are these people trained for? Certainly they are not worth 1/8th of a million £'s a year which is roughly what they are paid. It's very like medieval theologians endlessly debating how many angels can dance on the head of a pin. So I meekly took the jab and arranged to see them again with Chris next month. They need a fucking grenade up their arses to buck up their ideas.

I then had a very difficult funeral to go to. The daughter of the first shrink I was referred to and a family I had been at school with had drowned herself at sea after years and years of mental health treatment. 'Evidence based medicine' which all they aspire too implies they weren't very successful in treating her. It had seemed as if she was tired of being ill and all that involves, TAKE THIS, DON'T DO THAT, LISTEN TO OUR ADVICE. With her father being a psychiatrist it can only have made it worse by miles. Notably my mental health team didn't even mention the funeral or the stress it would involve. They were too busy deciding how many angels can dance on the end of a needle. To make it more difficult another even closer school friend had died of cancer at about the same time and she was very close to the family of the girl who drowned, Lesley so I had to break that news to them too. It was lovely seeing Lesley's sister Kate and we had a friendly argument about who was the biggest terror at school (she was by a long chalk) and we had a good hug. Chris came to the crematorium but I didn't manage to persuade him to come in sadly. He would have found the service interesting. So it's been a little frustrating all day. I should have liked to have had more time with Kate but Chris didn't want to meet up in the pub afterwards though the family invited everyone. I think I let Chris down a bit, but ever since I was denied the right to go to my own brother's funeral I have not been very confident about them.

Anyway its now 2.30 in the morning and we are just having a cuppa downstairs as we are both a bit restless. I guess it's all understandable but I do feel as though I could have achieved more today and I do think I was quite capable of having done so. Chris made every effort to accommodate me but I am left feeling up in the air. Guess its just grief although neither death affected me that deeply as I haven't seen either of them for years. If Chris had come to the funeral we would have been able to discuss it and I would get to know his views. It was just a bit of a cock up.

Now I have to say hello to some of my phantom readers because the authorities now have my URL so can read this whenever they want. I have always been aware of this, so I doubt the content will change or even perhaps if they will bother; after all they have those angels and pins to worry about and making plans for 10 years time when they may be persuaded to reduce my medication by 6.25 mg form 50 mgs.

Psychiatry kills, there is no question of that and they spend all their time discussing doses and threatening you if you don't take the medication. I'd die of boredom if I was them.

Ann Lawson

Sunday June 8, 2008 - 12:28am

Aldeburgh and my parents in Suffolk

Well today I am driving down to Aldeburgh to see Mum and Dad. Aldeburgh is famous for Benjamin Britten and the music festival and is a Suffolk town on the heritage coast. My daughter Tanya should be coming over from the farm and perhaps my brother Adrian later on. My parents have Ann Cartwright staying, an old school friend of my mothers who helped bring us kids up when we were small. She is also a social science statistician and had written several books. Mum and Dad have a sunny house with a large garden and dell, which Dad has planted up with a variety of trees. It is right by the golf course where they play nearly every day.

Dad is taking us all out to the Italian restaurant in town. I must remember to take my camera.

Friday June 13, 2008 - 12:54am

Great Italian meal in Aldeburgh with the family
Mum Tanya Ann Cartwright and Dad

Only You Can Cure Yourself

Sunday June 8, 2008 - 12:02am

52 things we should like to say at work

1. I can see your point, but I still think you're full of shit.

2. I don't know what your problem is, but I'll bet it's hard to pronounce.

3. How about never? Is never good for you?

4. I see you've set aside this special time to humiliate yourself in public.

5. I'm really easy to get along with once you people learn to see it my way.

6. Who lit the fuse on your tampon?

7. I'm out of my mind, but feel free to leave a message.

8. I don't work here. I'm a consultant.

9. It sounds like English, but I can't understand a word you're saying.

10. Ahhhh I see the fuck-up fairy has visited us again.

11. I like you. You remind me of myself when I was young and stupid.

12. You are validating my inherent mistrust of strangers.

13. I have plenty of talent and vision; I just don't give a shit.

14. I'm already visualizing the duct tape over your mouth.

15. I will always cherish the initial misconceptions I had about you.

16. Thank you. We're all refreshed and challenged by your unique point of view.

17. The fact that no one understands you doesn't mean you're an artist.

18. Any resemblance between your reality and mine are purely coincidental.

19. What am I? Flypaper for freaks?!

20. I'm not being rude. You're just insignificant.

21. It's a thankless job, but I've got a lot of Karma to burn off.

22. Yes, I am an agent of Satan, but my duties are largely ceremonial.

23. And your cry-baby whiny-arsed opinion would be?

24. Do I look like a fucking people person to you?

25. This isn't an office. It's Hell with fluorescent lighting.

26. I started out with nothing and I still have most of it left.

27. Sarcasm is just one more service we offer.

28. If I throw a stick, will you leave?

29. Errors have been made. Others will be blamed.

30. Whatever kind of look you were aiming for, you missed.

31. Oh I get it. Like humour, but different.........

32. An office is just a mental institute without the padded walls.

33. Can I swap this job for what's behind door.........?

34. Too many freaks, not enough circuses.

35. Nice perfume (or aftershave). Must you marinate in it?

36. Chaos, panic, and disorder. My work here is done.

37. How do I set a laser printer to stun?

38. I thought I wanted a career; it turns out I just needed the money.

39. I'll try being nicer if you'll try being more intelligent.

40. Wait a minute - I'm trying to imagine you with a personality.

41. Aren't you a black hole of need?

42. I'd like to help you out, which way did you come in?

43. Did you eat an extra bowl of stupid this morning?

44. Why don't you slip into something more comfortable? Like a coma.

45. If you have something to say raise your hand.........then place it over your mouth.

46. I'm too busy; can I ignore you some other time?

47. Don't let your mind wander; it's too small to be let out on its own.

48. Have a nice day, somewhere else.

49. You're not yourself today; I noticed the improvement straight away.

50. You are as pretty as a picture; I'd really like to hang you.

51. Don't believe everything you think.

52. Do you hear that? That's the sound of no-one caring.

Tuesday June 17, 2008 - 03:16pm

Ann Lawson

Entry for June 15, 2008

Well it was a very, very jolly day yesterday. We had the 80th celebration of the opening of our local park and I am vice chair of the committee. We only started planning in February so it has been very hard work. I was responsible for the Lord Mayor, two dragons and a load of other sundry dignitaries. Chris was chief umbrella holder to the lady Mayoress. I can't put into words the terrific time we had from 8.30 in the morning putting up balloons and bunting till 6.00 at night packing up. I lost 5lbs and the committee made £50 profit. Everyone said what a success it was and how much they enjoyed it and we are all on a massive high :) It was also very funny.

I had a lovely weekend relaxing at Chris's. It's great to get out of the city, although I do live in the suburbs where it is quite quiet and everyone keeps there gardens nicely. This is a 1951 council house, which my Dad bought for me for £46,000 on the open market in 1992. It was cheaply built, but well designed and spacious. It's also a good neighbourhood and the 'friends of the park 'are helping to improve it. It's worth about £170,000 now. The garden is looking good at the moment. To get colour in the summer you have to plant annuals and biennials. My daughter has been up several times recently and commented on how nice the garden looks. My plan is to stuff it with plants so all the weeds are strangled, :)

Wednesday June 18, 2008 - 04:09am

72

Vermeer...what total accomplishment!

Vermeer is a Dutch interior painter renowned for his use of light. His mastery is totally apparent when you see his work in situ. Read 'the girl with the pearl earring'

Row, row, row your boat, gently down the stream. Merrily, merrily, merrily, merrily life is but a dream

Fox and Goose Inn Fressingfield Suffolk

We all had a wonderfully jolly lunch at the Fox and Goose in Suffolk, though it must have cost Dad a deposit on a small house. It has been years since I have seen my aunt and Uncle and I was quite nervous but it was all enjoyable and the food was delicious. It was Mum and Dad's diamond wedding anniversary. Tanya was there, as were most of my youngest brother's family, but my other brother was in Tunisia and of course my sister was in New Zealand. Actually my sister was a bit old maidish when I phoned her on Sunday to say how it went. I was laughing a lot and she asked me 'have you been smoking dope?!'

Ann Lawson

Sunday July 13, 2008 - 07:17pm

Thursday July 3, 2008 - 03:54pm

Entry for July 02, 2008

I am just getting back to work after feeling really exhausted after the Park celebrations.

I have started doing interviews for the Norwich Living History project of old people's memories. I did my first yesterday. The chair lady of the project is a great friend of mine.

I am also back working for the mental health trust in the service users' council and have offered to do two days on the interview panel for a co-ordinator for old people's services.

We also have some family luncheons coming up. This Sunday Chris and I are having lunch in a Suffolk pub with my younger brother and his wife. And next Saturday we are having lunch in another famous Suffolk pub with my parents, my father's brother and his wife, my younger brother and his wife (again) and my daughter Tanya. My elder brother has gone off to Tunisia for a week with his family, which I think will be unbearably hot this time of year.

My daughter has moved into a caravan in a country area and started her teaching job yesterday. If she completes the year she will have totally completed her training. She is hoping her boyfriend, Reinier, will find a job in London and come and join her so they can afford more permanent accommodation. However London is a deep contrast to safari-leading in Africa which is what he was doing when she met him. At the moment he is still in Ireland. She rather likes her caravan so far. She has another car too courtesy of her ever-obliging mother. However that probably means I won't be going on holiday in September, as I won't have enough money, especially with the stock market as it is.

Anyway that's all my news. I'm trying to get back into the rhythm of things and discipline myself to keep quite active. The park celebrations took up most of my time for at least three months. However it was a massive success.

Wednesday July 2, 2008 - 01:06pm

Nelson Mandela is 90

There was a concert in London tonight to celebrate and promote Mandela's charity 46664; named after his prison number. After years spent in hospital on and off I can empathise with people incarcerated.

Friday August 15, 2008

Stopping smoking
Smoke free zone

Sunday August 10, 2008

Ann Lawson

Stopping smoking

Well I haven't smoked since my weekly meeting with my stop smoking counsellor last Thursday which is three and a half days. I'm using Nicorette patches and a Nicorette inhalator and have read two stop-smoking books on top of my councillor's advice. The cravings are definitely more manageable now and after a few weeks of no smoking on the Nicorette substitutes I should be eventually able to go bareback. I think you have to be properly motivated before you try to stop (I was very conscious of my health suffering), then the counsellor, Katie, a lovely woman, has been invaluable and finally the nicotine substitute takes the edge off the battle. But Nicotine is a worthy opponent and will try all the tricks in the world just to make you smoke that one, which will undo your quit. It is very similar to being an alcoholic on the 12-step programme; you cannot have even one drink. However I did have to go my own pace and started with just cutting down to about 7 a day. Now I am smoke clean but still have a low level of nicotine, which is the addictive drug that keeps us smoking. Every cigarette is just to relieve the withdrawal symptoms the last cigarette left. But also in every cigarette of every sort there are 4000 toxic chemicals and insecticides. That's apart from the carbon monoxide smoking packs your blood with. Katie measures mine every week and I saw a dramatic drop the first week and then about the same level the next week on reduced consumption, so this week I hope to be clear.

I am much more full of energy, my mouth feels tons better, my lungs aren't so painful, and surprisingly I find I have much more free time now I'm not spending every other ten minutes smoking a 10 minute cigarette. So in effect even with time management apart from lack of cravings, I am much less stressed! Then of course I have more money, although I had always bought my baccy cheaply.

All is very well, but Chris is still smoking and though he has been very supportive it has proved very hard for me to quit without him. He isn't smoking in my presence which is very good of him but it has been an uphill struggle to do it on your own without your nearest and dearest joining in. The counsellor has helped there. Also I have had loads of support from my friends and family. However insurance companies don't classify you as a 'non-smoker' till you haven't smoked for a year so that is my goal at the moment. Most people say, though, 'take each day at a time'.

Sunday August 10, 2008 - 04:04pm

Beijing Olympics

Today is the first day of the Beijing Olympics and rather than moan about China's human rights record like Bush who hasn't got much to boast about himself, I think we should give China a chance and wish them good luck. It is a proud nation emerging from an ancient and feudal tradition into a rapidly expanding and fascinating country. The Chinese people themselves are excited by the prospect of such an enormous venture and it is just bad cheese to keep on carping about human rights, which upsets many Chinese people. They have experienced terrible suffering under Mao, now its time for us to congratulate them on the progress they have made since. I feel kind of envious that they have a government which can put on such an effort and then again I'm cautious that it is not just another dictatorship like the Berlin games. However I admire there enthusiasm which is in contrast to British tired cynicism.

Friday August 8, 2008 - 01:43am

Stopping smoking

I went to see a specialist stop smoking advisor on the NHS yesterday, called Katie, a very nice woman. She advised me to start wearing the patches and use the inhalator at the same time. I would have probably tried quitting long ago with all the new smoking restrictions if I hadn't been with Chris who smokes heavily and won't even discuss giving up. So I explained this to the advisor and she said it was achievable but would definitely be harder. She also gave me a leaflet on smoking and mental health. The figures are alarming, 70% at least of service users smoke compared to 26% of the general population. There is a whole culture of smoking amongst service users which is reinforced by the staff in hospital.

I am at the moment going for harm reduction, that is to say, although I am wearing the patches and it is making a lot of difference to how much I smoke and using the inhalator to top it up, yet I am still smoking occasionally, but the urge is not so strong.

Every time I wake up I am conscious of how ill I feel from smoking; shortness of breath, foul tasting mouth and chest pains. I have ordered four books off of Amazon on giving up so I am all set. May be I shall be smoke free soon. I am going to see Katie again next Friday. Wish me luck.

When some rogue married me for a couple of years (long divorced and dead) when I was ill still, my daughter took the opportunity to attach herself to my brother Robert and his wife and family. They live in an Elizabethan mansion on the farm in Suffolk. It is idyllic and much more fun than living with poor old Mum. Anyway she can gossip and snipe and bitch about me and Granny to her heart's content and they all feel dreadfully sorry for her. I have done my best to woo her back with love, care, attention and massive amounts of money but nothing works. I have even spoken to our solicitor and farm secretary. Now I have written a courteous note to the Lawson family at Hill House which is where they live, asking them to do their part. They are on holiday at the moment but perhaps they will see sense. There doesn't seem to be anything else I can do.

Only You Can Cure Yourself

Sunday August 31, 2008

Lovely weekend

I went over to Chris and we spent the afternoon shopping in Holt, then sunbathing nude in his garden and getting up to naughty things (totally private there :)).

On Sunday Chris drove my car to Holkham beach and we walked to a quiet place in the dunes. I was hoping to swim on the nudist beach there but the tide was out so I just stripped off in the warmth. Chris took some tasteful photos...
Then I managed to make contact with my daughter and some sort of peace after the terrible time I have had for the last two weeks. At least she got it off her chest and hasn't changed her number.

Chris is off to London tomorrow to move his son into his new flat for the next term at University. He is doing very well, particularly for someone who was diagnosed with Asperger syndrome not so many years ago.

I have booked another holiday in Tenerife late October.

Friday August 29, 2008

Crime

I noticed a couple of days ago that bricks were being thrown in my garden. Then I heard an air pistol discharge. Rather than call 999 and get sectioned by the damn police, I contacted the neighbourhood watch warden who is a friend of mine. The lad who lives in the house at the bottom of my garden was picked up nearby with a machete and air pistol in breach of bail and so is now in prison. Naturally I feel a lot safer now. I was quite scared and confused.

Thursday August 28, 2008

Eaton Park

Four of us friends of Eaton Park are going to a park in Great Yarmouth today to see another park that has green flag status which means we will be entitled to some money for nature and habitat improvements; hopefully bird boxes. Although I put a bird box in my garden this year, none nested there. But there are an abundance of birds in the garden who are untroubled by the neighbour's cat now who never comes over any more. I have put some fat out for them from a hock I bought and it hasn't gone rancid, so I suppose they are enjoying that.

The end of the world

Well many people predicted the end of the world today, as the scientists were trying out a new particle collider or something. But at 8.30 we were all still here (I think) and I was at the GP with Chris having my annual check up, which went OK. Then I picked up my prescription and posted a stop smoking book to a friend and bought some reading glasses for a friend in Hospital. Then Chris and I walked back here for a break and a sit down. Then Chris drove me, in my car to the hospital to visit Rowena/Clare and drop off the reading glasses. We sat in the garden and watched the birds and planes. She is trying to tunnel out! Then Chris and I did some shopping and I bought my sweeteners and Chris took the bus home and I drove.

I am interviewing my old (previous and old) head mistress at the Great Hospital on Monday for our Living History project so I am going over to Sarah's to pick up a voice recorder tomorrow evening.

Wednesday September 10, 2008 - 07:53am

Adversity

I applied to be an admissions/ registrar at my old school this weekend and spent a lot of time filling in the application form. I was totally qualified and would have made a good job of it but had a terse e-mail this morning say I had been rejected even though the closing date was only yesterday. They seemed to be desperate to disappoint me.

It appears my daughter HAS got an address. She told me she hadn't an address at her caravan in Essex, so when her birthday card for August the 3rd from her grandparents came here I wasn't sure what to do with it especially as she doesn't like me phoning her. So in the end I forwarded it to her aunt and uncle in Suffolk hoping they would invite her to stay and she would get it. Her aunt and uncle then went to the Canaries for a holiday so yesterday when they returned I phoned them and it turns out there is an address but you have to send mail via her friend in Manchester where she was at university. This friend has an alcoholic husband and two children and lives in a council house so I was kind of concerned about mail going there, not that I had the address. Any way they had forwarded the mail to Manchester before they went on holiday and I phoned Tanya last night and she had received it and said 'why are you bothering me?'

Not really surprising I didn't get the job I hoped to get.

Sunday September 7, 2008 - 10:53pm

Gardening Party

Today we are cutting the bottom hedge for the first time since 1992, and then we will be able to see our new neighbours. I have a skip out the front and have had the gate fixed and fixed the brick in the wall of the shed. Chris is bringing two band saws. Judith Lubbock the lib dem councillor has bought some clippers and I have made a small foray into the undergrowth and looked at what is beyond the hedge. I hope my Dutch friend Hank is coming and Eva our home watch person is coming this afternoon. Sylvie my German friend has offered to lend a chain saw, which will be useful to cut the branches into smaller bits. Possibly other people will help when they see us at it. We have the skip till Friday so there is plenty of time. The neighbours might even help.
Monday September 8, 2008 - 09:43pm

We successfully cut the hedge

We successfully cleared the bottom of the garden. Not with many people but those who did help were brilliant. I am very pleased with the result and although it was an exhausting day it was very satisfying. One neighbour even brought round hot Hungarian meat balls and pancakes to feed us after the job was complete. It was a very lovely Sunday.

Entry for September 01, 2008

Harvest is over for the year except for some drying. My brother Adrian took his family to London to see a show, to celebrate.

Friday Walkers

Every Friday morning, come rain or shine I go for a walk in Eaton Park next door with a varied group of people.

Monday September 29, 2008 - 03:40pm

Visit home

Well I finally persuaded Chris that I needed to visit my parents and we had a great visit. It was lovely to see Mum and Dad (and the sea at Aldeburgh). I have been rushed off my feet recently with Chris retiring and work and socialising. Today we left Mum and Dad at 8.00 to go model aeroplane flying.

This is a picture by Ingres of Isabelle de Broglie who died of consumption (TB) in the 19th century and whose husband kept her painting behind shrouds for the rest of his life. It now hangs in the metropolitan museum in USA. The de Broglie's are the family I stayed with when I was 19. In 1929 one of them got the Nobel Prize for Physics. I had no idea when I went who they were though they knew me. It was like being sent off to service in a wealthy family and being a servant because I did not realise our family had personal contact with them. That is why I got ill. It wasn't until Mum told me in 2002 who it was I was staying with that I finally made the connection (over 30 years later). The repercussions have been huge on my illness but I am OK now.

Sunday September 28, 2008 - 05:39pm

Entry for September 21, 2008

I have had a tough time recently, giving up smoking and then taking it up again. However things seem to be levelling out. My Mum and Dad hopefully came back from a holiday in Italy yesterday (the Italian airline crisis permitting) and Chris and I hope to stay with them on Saturday night on the way to fly model aeroplanes again; what else! Dad has been asking to see me for a while and Chris has been so worried about me he wouldn't let me go. So it should be a great meeting. People say I am looking well at the moment. They say 'Chris must be doing you good'.

Ann Lawson

Steam train from Liverpool Street at Norwich Station

Chris and I and Les Hopkins met the Oliver Cromwell arriving from London in Norwich. The drivers looked very tired and their faces were covered in soot.

Sunday September 21, 2008 - 12:21pm

My old headmistress

I interviewed my old headmistress, Miss Bartholomew, for our Norwich Living history group yesterday. I did everything right but forgot to press record!

She was born in Clapham in 1913 and had a brother and a sister. Her father was a gold book embellisher. Her grandfather owned a shop in Scotland. They used to travel up by train to visit him. She is a Methodist. She won a scholarship to a school in Westminster and got a 2.1 at University in English and History. She had a teaching job with the Girls'Public Day School Trust in London and then was offered a headship with The Norwich High School GPDST in 1951. First she lived on Bluebell Road; then in the close at Hooks Walk and at the moment she is at Elaine Herbert House, The Great Hospital, Bishopgate, Norwich because she has broken her femur.

She has always loved Norwich, its history and the Maddermarket Theatre, and though she was offered promotion, she turned it down because she did not want to leave Norwich.

I took her a bunch of Flowers. It was lovely to see her again. She almost remembered me, which is saying something!!!! But she remembered my sister.

Entry for November 03, 2008

Chris and I are happy again, I hope. We spent a great Sunday together and I cooked gammon and pineapple. I have returned from holiday with renewed fortitude and strength and am taking problems in my stride. My Mum and Dad are coming up to Norwich on Thursday because Dad wants to buy Mum a new outfit then we are going to lunch in the local farmhouse pub. Dad is considering planning a holiday in the Canary Islands, :)

I want to go to Paris in the spring, perhaps for my birthday, in April. I have found a cheap trip with Eurostar and a small hotel at £190 per person sharing for three days. But I can't get anyone to go with me! Any offers?

I have the service user's council at Hellesdon tomorrow which I am a member of, then a Spanish class in the evening at Hellesdon High School.

It is supposed to be a stupendous autumn for leaf colour and it certainly seems to be so. We have the nomination forms for Friends of Eaton Park through and I hope to stand as vice chair again.

Monday November 3, 2008 - 04:37pm

Holiday

I've just got back from another week in Tenerife. I was getting very depressed and it really cheered me up. The weather was a bit damp, but I did some swimming and sunbathing. It was a lovely hotel; lots of English people who were very friendly and helpful. I met a lot of rich English widows who spend their time holidaying and enjoying life. On wet days I took one of the local buses to see the island. This is a picture of Mount Teide, which is an extinct volcano and the highest mountain in Spain.

Back home I can see why I was getting depressed...Chris is so boring and unsupportive and has taken up sexual DIY and my family is all so right wing.

Anyway I am hoping to sue the city outreach team (mental health idiots) for negligence and also am going to apply for another job (yet again).

Only You Can Cure Yourself

Wednesday October 29, 2008 - 11:48pm

Butterfly kisses

Woke up this morning thinking of the butterfly kisses I used to give my daughter when she was a baby. Also, Ann Cartwright gave her some toys and I used to blow on her face with this rubber egg. It was yellow. I would massage her with baby oil and she slept in a Moses basket at the top of my bed. I watched as she slept to make sure she was still alive. Butterfly kisses are when you flutter your eyelashes against someone, brushing their skin. I used to bath her in the sink but even at that age she would try and reach the cups hanging there. A ship went down in Felixstowe when she was small and lives were lost, I think. It was only a few yards from where we were living. I listened to it on the radio and one of my neighbours went out to see if he could help. It was a P&O roll of roll on. That is the Lorries roll off and on. She had croup when she was small and the doctor advised me to boil a kettle in the room. I put her in her rain buggy and put the kettle under the canopy. She is lucky she didn't end up a lobster. The doctor thought I was a good Mum and I was. We were really close and I never left her with anyone if I could help it. Her father used to come round and so did her grandparents. But then when I moved house they took her away.

Chris

I have been going out with Chris for almost three years now. He's a nice enough man and very well read. We had our differences but had a pretty good time together all told. Sometimes we had terrific fun especially in the early years. However, prompted by someone on the net I said something wrong and now what ever I say he won't have me back again. We talk endlessly but the physical side is non existent and also I rarely see him. I've done everything in my power to apologise and put it right but he is a very unforgiving man. I think he gets it from his mother. Her mother put her in an orphanage with her sister when their father died in the war. She took them out later and did everything she could to make it up to them but Chris's mother never forgave her own mother and according to Chris this scarred her for life. Chris has trouble with relationships too and ours has lasted longer than he is used to, particularly as we don't live together. However I have to accept it's over.

I am saddened not only to lose him but that the world is such a flawed place that after putting so much effort into a relationship a tiny error, which I have apologised for, he cannot for give me for. My faith in humanity is somewhat shattered which is perhaps what he intends as he must judge all women by his mother and however much he says he hated her he must have loved her quite a lot. So now I have a man who I have invested my whole life history in and he doesn't want to play with me any more. It's quite a blow and I am depressed. It took me at least six months to find Chris and I introduced him to all my family but he seems to be determined to hurt me as much as possible. He says he is not a Christian and I can well believe it. It's a nasty underhand thing for him to do.

So all you intelligent good looking men out there I'm on the scrap heap and need resurrecting. I'm not bitter although I am depressed and I shall be more circumspect in future. I'm not a great catch I know. My illness has taken its toll and I am still buggered about by the mental health authorities. But as they say I do have 'big tits'! (This is a side effect of the drugs) That's about my only claim to fame these days.

I'm on the look out. I am interested in anyone who is educated to degree level or beyond. Local would be best and I don't fancy being

a mistress. I'm not into sharing. I enjoy travelling and music and the radio. I hate the television and I enjoy walking and swimming. I smoke. I'm politically left field and try and keep informed. I enjoy foreign holidays and solitude. I think sex is a healthy activity and, if good, the cement of a relationship. I just want a loving relationship with a physical side as well. Is that too much to ask? So come on boys...speak up and give me something to be cheerful about this Christmas.
Thursday December 4, 2008 - 05:56pm

Christmas round-robin

Many people hate round robins but I thought I would attempt one this year. I have been to Tenerife from Norwich twice this year. Once in February when the weather was good, and then again in October, when the weather was a little wet. I studied a little Spanish the second time I went and enjoyed using that. It's a great destination as you can fly from Norwich but with the pound so low at the moment I won't be going again in a hurry. The destinations they recommend now are Mexico, South Africa, Iceland and Turkey where the pound is still holding its own. Still I am planning to go to stay with a French friend of mine in the spring near Paris. Then perhaps I'll save up for Mexico or South Africa.

It's been a very sad year for losing friends. Kathy Lawrance who was my best friend at school died of non specific Hodgkinsons disease in the spring and a week later Lesley Abel whose father was a psychiatrist and had the bad luck to be a mental patient drowned herself at sea. She was probably in the class above Ruth at school. Meantime two great friends have died of natural causes incredibly young, so it really has been a series of funerals. Even the man on the fruit and vegetable van who sold me tobacco died of a heart attack. Perhaps I am just a Jonah ☹

I have been working for the service user's council at the hospital which is an entertaining rabble, run by a drunkard. Also I have been active in friends of Eaton Park as vice chair and we had a terrific open day this year which the Lord Mayor came to (and I had to look after). I have also been interviewing people for their memories of Norwich for archiving for a living history project run by a great friend of mine. I got to interview my old head mistress, which was great fun but forgot to press the record button. It was nice to see her again even if she didn't remember me at all. She remembered Ruth though!

I have been going out with Chris Holford for nearly three years. He is a retired further education physics teacher who has moved to Holt after a divorce and retirement. We explore the north Norfolk coast and do daft things like make sloe gin and crab apple jelly. Chris is a terrific model aeroplane designer and builder and about three times a year drags me off to Shuttleworth College in Bedfordshire for an open day. It's all a bit old men in dirty raincoats with pebble glasses but they love it and it keeps them out of trouble. Even Mum and Dad and their solicitor met us there for an air display of old, full size planes.

I decided to be a bit ambitious and reach for the dizzying heights of chair of friends of Eaton park this year and was just getting to limber up for the contest and my brother Adrian slams on the brakes which left me screaming in frustration for several weeks. However I was so depressed at the fiasco he caused I might be able to wangle a reduction in some of my medication.

Other news Ruth has swapped Peter for a better house with a view and Adrian's daughter Bethany is back at school after Adrian felt it appropriate to put her in an adolescent unit for two years. He now fancies himself as the mental health Tzar.

I am still in the same house I have been in since 1992, and it is beginning to feel like home. I have a lot of good friends (those that are still alive) and walk a lot and swim when on holiday. I'm still on the nicotine weed though I gave up for 10 days this summer. My weight is not sylph like but it is constant and I've not been hospitalised for over two years now. Not much of an achievement and I realise as a late developer I am leaving it a bit late to get on "I'm a celebrity get me out of here." But on the whole I'm just happy to have cleared up the confusion in my mind which had lasted 30 years and to have my confidence back. I've felt well since 2002 and despite constant frays and struggles that feeling of loving and being loved has stayed with me.

Tanya looks to Robert and Shellee as her guardians now and I am sure they do a good job. Last I heard she was living in a caravan and doing her final qualifying year as a teacher in Essex. She has done an enormous amount of travelling since university.

Mum and Dad are fit and healthy and seem to still be actively enjoying retirement.

Anyway that is the end of my round robin thing. Hope it wasn't too boring. If you need the Samaritans number after reading it it's probably on the Christmas card.

I wish you all a happy and balanced New Year and a boozy Christmas.

Sunday November 30, 2008 - 10:54pm

Injections

I may have finally convinced my father who is regularly on the phone to the authorities that injections are not the only way to administer medication, I am going to refuse them from now on and ask for some cheap pill substitutes.

Entry for November 22, 2008

Well, a lot has happened. I took my computer into a shop for them to speed it up and they totally burnt out my hard drive. So I have had to buy a new computer and have lost 10 years of data. I keep on meeting very nice men but my brother (another of the animals in my family) put me down before I went on holiday and returned me to my sick bed I have had no luck in love. Fortunately Chris still talks to me a bit but I feel I am wasting opportunities as usual and have taken a giant step backwards in my recovery. This is the elder of my two younger brothers who recently put his 14-year-old daughter in mental hospital. So he is quite a charming character and now he has started on me. He has been avoiding Chris and me all year despite lots of invitations.

Saturday November 22, 2008 - 03:45pm

Poorly

I have been quite ill recently and eventually had to call my community psychiatric nurse round. They diagnosed lack of sleep so I made sure I slept well last night. I still feel a bit nervous but they are going to come round once a week for a few weeks till I am settled again. Chris isn't well either and has a bad cold but hopefully we can both get better together and continue to give each other support. Otherwise things are OK. I must get down to some reading; not done any in ages... and generally keep busy. I have put a bit of weight on whilst I was ill so must get rid of that too. Looking at my previous blog I wonder how much my naughty daughter was to blame! Mum and Dad have been great as usual. Chris has excelled himself too despite being ill himself... Despite my lack of sleep I do feel re-energized after my holiday and I am very glad I made the effort to go.

Happy New Year

Well I made it through Christmas and I would describe it as interesting. Quite stressful at times and dangerous but I'm still living and breathing and most importantly at home and not in an institution.

A very happy New Year to all my friends. Let's hope it's a better one.

Friday January 9, 2009

Just back from France

Had a great time with Joel in Paris. Well worth all the hard work.

Loose Screw

One wrong note

Only You Can Cure Yourself

Dad drove me slowly along Buckingham Road, "See how well kept all the gardens are. Your house could look as nice as your neighbour's next door"

It was cheap-brick semi-detached house on a council estate. "I wonder how long it will take for Ann to turn it into a slum" he asides to Mum.

"I don't like it" I confess to Mum. "But your father is buying it for you." Mum decides the matter.

I had never wanted to live on an estate or in a council house especially a privatised one, being vehemently anti-Thatcher and the sale of council houses. In the pub they say "Your daddy bought you a house didn't he". I was 41 with a 10 –year- old daughter.

The first night in the house Tanya was hungry and I had nothing. Andy was there but for some reason I didn't ask him to go out for fish and chips and he didn't offer. I made Tanya drink some sour milk to fill her tummy. She fell down the stairs later and bumped her head. I was so determined to do the right thing I made her stay in hospital in case of concussion. It was her birthday the next day. She spent it in hospital.

Andy had been my boyfriend since I moved to Norwich in 1984. I met him in the local loony bin. He had one trouser leg tucked into his sock as he queued at the hatch for his breakfast and I thought 'what a mess!' I used to sit and hold his hand because he was so sorry-looking but also perhaps the only person with any education amongst the patients. He was a dentist. Much later on he told me he had tried to throw him self down the stairs in the hospital and had ECT. I never had ECT thank God.

Tanya and I settled down to a quiet life in our new nondescript house. Her school was just over the road and I took a job as dinner lady at another school, and then I did a postgraduate course in administration ("boring!" as a friend said recently.) On the strength of the course I got a job at the local hospital for the disabled as a volunteer's co-ordinator. I had to recruit and supervise volunteers to help the nurses and organised trips out for those able enough to go.

I had an office of my own and would quickly finish any paper work. Then I would help Reg fill in his betting slips for the horses. He had no movement at all except for a slight sideways motion of his head. I would stand behind him as he sat in his chair.

The hospital was less than a mile away but I always took my car, white and battered with one blue wing. I was very proud and happy to have a job. A lot of it was thanks to my tutor from when I was at Bristol University who was very supportive on the phone.

Things seemed to be fairly settled and normal. Tanya spent all her time watching television and flew into a total rage if I turned it off and put some music on. I would try and talk to her but she would ignore me. I took to watching the back of the telly. She was doing well at school and I was working. Mum and Dad liked Andy and he would drop by whenever he felt like it. He was company. I felt independent and in control. I was on injections of antipsychotics I remember as not long afterwards I was to stop them.

One day when I was confidently leaving my office feeling all professional and smart, a colleague came up to me and said "I have something to tell you. Andy and I are going out together. He didn't want you to know."

I went home early. Phoned an old friend and had a drink with him, then lay down in the kitchen with my head in the dog basket and cried my eyes out. I left the job soon afterwards.

One wrong note

I had struggled against mental health treatment for years...since 1975 and before. But my parents were very keen for me to have it and most of the doctors agreed with them. Consequently I was in and out of hospital like a yo-yo, loathing every minute of it. I spent most of my time running away and trying to settle in new towns incognito with a new job until my past caught up with me and I'd be back in hospital. I wanted to get as far away from my parents as possible. When I had Tanya she was repeatedly put in foster homes when I was in hospital. The whole thing was a nightmare. I took a many overdoses. The pill-taking had first started at university when I split up with the man I was living with.

I went over every detail of my life trying to find a cause as I rarely had classic mental illness symptoms. It wasn't till I was totally on my own and out of luck that I threw myself into facing up to what I was frightened off. Tanya had reached the conclusion in her counselling she received that the main problem was that I didn't get on with my parents, so I took that as my starting point. But that wasn't until 2002.

One wrong note

Tanya and I usually had lodgers in the house. Our latest was Nick; a postgraduate student at the university who was suicidal and frightened he would end up an alcoholic. He was a member of some far-left political group. We got on well and he helped me start writing. I decided not to have any more lodgers but moved in a partner whom I could sleep with. I thought it would be as uncomplicated as that.

Jim had been married to Tish, Tanya and I had known them from the parties they had at their place with their thousands of grown up kids and cats and friends. Tish was a farmer's daughter and Jim had a large beer belly and very long grey hair like a woman's. He had this hat with all different badges on it such as 'ban the bomb.' He was a typical Norwich ageing hippy but with a cruel sense of humour. He also had an unknown number of children, grandchildren and great grandchildren. I had worked with Tish his wife on a community education project for the Open University. Tish left Jim and about a year later he was living in a rented cottage by Whitlingham Broad on the East of the city. Tanya and I went down there one evening. Jim immediately moved away from the girl he was going out with at the time and took me upstairs. Tanya slept in his dressing cupboard and Jim made love to me. The next morning I noticed my gold ring I had placed on the bedstead had gone and whilst we searched for it Jim asked me to marry him. Crying my eyes out in distress I accepted. I don't know if it was the same day but Jim was booking our engagement party in the local pub and the police turned up and arrested him. Apparently they had been looking for him for several years for fraud.

I think my thought processes must have been extremely disordered but I carried on supporting him even when he went to court and then prison. His friends and family started coming to my house and I had his dog and would spend endless hours playing ball with her in the kitchen until I couldn't stand it any longer. I asked Nick the lodger to visit him in prison after a while instead of me. I told his family I wanted to chuck him but they wouldn't allow me to whilst he was in prison.

He arrived outside my house with a bunch of flowers one day. I gave him a cup of tea and said no way could he stay. He said the prison authorities would section me unless I allowed him. So I said just for a few days. He didn't leave until he had ruined my house, upset Tanya and my parents, stolen all my valuable keepsakes and pawned them for drink and then married me. I forgot we were getting married on the day conveniently but he made me phone up and arrange it for the next day. I was getting very run down. My teeth were falling out. He would come back from the pub at 11.30 and wake me up then read until two so, being an early riser, I got no sleep. He would then lie in bed until 2.00pm. It was like having an enormous terrifying parasite in the house. I moved out (of my own house) and into a flat. Tanya was put in care and I was arrested. I was held in a cell, interviewed in the police station by two psychiatrists then held in a cage until they were ready to take me in a police van, with about 12 police men to the hospital, where all the nurses were lined up to greet me and of course inject me.

One wrong note

Jim and I were married for about 2 years and lived together for less than that. Dad thought Jim wanted the house. He moved all his stuff in and his dog. He never cut the lawn or the hedges and grew what he called 'water melons' in the garden, which turned out to be marrows. We bought a long dining table which we put in the living room and sat each side. He would start telling a story, with no beginning or end, and would get more fanciful by the minute. So I would go out; but I didn't like leaving him in the house because I knew he was selling all mine and Tanya's possessions; from the valuable jewellery her father bought when I was pregnant to a 3,000 year old stone axe head we had discovered together by the university lake when out walking. He even set up a trade in second hand books, robbing the recycling bins outside, and taking some of mine, then selling them to book shops.

My reputation in the area slumped so tradesmen would not even come to the house. If Jim cleared up the dog shit in the garden he threw it over the hedge into the neighbour's garden. Beer cans would go that way too. He bought a pair of Vietnamese pot bellied pigs and these two brothers rooted around in the garden destroying everything. I made a sty for them in the shed and sometimes when things got too much for me in the house I would go there and talk to them.

Things often got too much for me and I would go and sit in the park or take one of the series of broken down vehicles he bought and drive up to Manchester or over to France. I felt I was being forced out of my own house and he had taken over.

I missed Tanya terribly but the violence in the house was too severe to try and get her back. Moreover I wasn't sure she wanted to come back.

I often collected all his possessions together and made an enormous pile of them in the middle of the living room, trying to get him to leave. In the end I stopped sleeping in the same room as him and he then moved into the little room. Soon after that, when I was in hospital, he and a friend backed a van up to the front door and emptied the house of everything. He moved into a council flat and never came back. He died of a heart attack in his sleep, January 26th 2005.

Beginning

I had an idyllic childhood or at least a very lucky one, being brought up on a farm in Suffolk with 4 brothers and sisters and lots of people coming and going and staying. Mum always said I would be a 'blue stocking' and I certainly worked very hard at school and enjoyed it. Primary school was easy. In secondary school we went away to Norwich and boarded during the week in lodgings. It was an excellent school - all girls. My brothers went to the cathedral school in Norwich.

I loved the six form and did History and history of art, English and Latin for A level and music appreciation at A/O level at the same time. I was editor of the school magazine but never a prefect. My sister Ruth won a scholarship to Imperial College London to read Zoology.

When it came time for me to apply to University, along with about 10 of my classmates, I was asked if I wanted to apply to Oxford and Cambridge as my first choices. Up until then my life had been normal within reason but now I was to go off the rails.

Before I got my results for A-levels, Mum and Ruth had a talk with me and said I should take a holiday in France. I was quite cross as all I wanted to do was to read in preparation for Oxbridge entrance next term. I knew I had a lot of work to do and I was VERY excited. I must have been to make such a hash of things. I never asked whom I would be staying with in France. I just thought "I'll get this job over then get down to work."

The family sent me the tickets and I flew to Geneva, a lovely flight, and landed at a small airport. The family were all waiting to greet me but I kept a very professional distance. I thought it was just another job. I usually had taken basic jobs during the holidays to be independent of the family since I was 14 and even worked abroad (in Italy.) However this wasn't working out as I wanted. I wasn't popular with the kids or the mother. They seemed not to want me there. I got friendly with one of the other nannies and used to hit the dance spots at night. I was getting very tired working days and going out nights. Also the mother seemed to give me more and more demeaning work to do and my position at the meal table, which had always been with the servants (although other servants waited on us), was reduced to sitting with the children. I hardly spoke to the family and though the father was nice to me on occasions (he gave me some chocolate) I was very lonely, unhappy and ill. I wrote a postcard to my parents in desperation saying "this is just a boring Summer holiday" but naturally got no reply because that is exactly what they thought it was; a holiday. They had no idea until 33 years later that I hadn't a clue who I was staying with.

Meantime Mum sent me my A level results and I had an A, B and a C plus a distinction in History of Art and in music.

I was washing the children's clothes out in the open under a cold tap without soap when finally I broke and decided that I would look for comfort elsewhere. So I slept with the French lothario who had been chasing me. I was very much a virgin. The following morning my aeroplane tickets to Italy to stay with my grandparents were due so the father drove me to the airport and I flew to Italy. Granny and Granddad were all over the place as that morning the Italian who had been politely courting me, whenever I visited them, drove his car over a cliff near their home. I think my mind closed down. I didn't recover until I found out who the family were in 2002; the mystery grew to bug me so much.

One wrong note

I went back to school for the extra term Oxbridge students did then but was out of the habit of reading and still suffering from tiredness. I put my misunderstanding with the French mother down to a language problem. She had told me off for going out at night and leaving the shutters open which the Mistral (the north wind in the south) had banged and woken the grandmother. I said "je suis sensible" but when I came home I found the correct translation was "I am sensitive". I got a postcard from the French lothario with no address which just said "souviens les etoiles"; "remember the stars". We used to lie out under them at night and he gave me his jumper to keep warm. My Mum said "I don't like that jumper." I just couldn't understand where my mother was coming from any more.

We were all sat round the kitchen table at Bullocks Hill Farm where Dad had started farming and the letter from Oxford was there. I had applied to Lady Margaret Hall. It was a rejection. I had never failed an exam in my life before although I only got border line on the 11 plus. No one seemed to mind or care but I was devastated. What the hell was I going to do now? All my friends who had applied had been accepted at Oxford or Cambridge. I had been awarded the school history prize that year.

I took a job in the local stationery shop (books, fags, pens and magazines) in the nearest market town about 9 miles away. I had no transport and hitched in morning and night even in the winter. I was paid £9 a week. I wasn't allowed to read but had to serve the customers, polish the doorknocker and dust. One day my headmistress phoned the shop and said she had arranged an interview at Oxford for me. I just knew it wasn't going to be successful when I was doing a job like that and I wasn't successful although I went over in my mind for years afterwards what I had said or rather not said.

I worked at the shop for four months often hitching back in the dark. Then I was made redundant. At the time I was teaching myself to type in Dad's office at night in the hope of going to America as a secretary and now joined the technical college in Ipswich and did a typing course. I wasn't allowed to take any exams so I joined Eastern electricity just outside Ipswich through an agency. The work was so mindlessly boring I collapsed and then went up to the personnel officer to ask for a better job and he transferred me to his department. I wrote one or two reports. He suggested I didn't go to university but stay there in a better job. I was travelling up by train by this time and had a small car I bought for £25, which caught fire on the way home but served me well until it blew up from lack of oil.

However I wasn't going to abandon my university career totally and was attracted to moving to the sea as everyone who is ill does.

I left Eastern Electricity and moved into a caravan in Aldeburgh, working in a pub behind the bar. Mum thought I was lonely and sent my two great friends Richard Keys and Kathy Lawrance to stay with me. I wasn't too pleased as I had quite an active sex life by this time, which I had to put on hold.

Kathy persuaded us to all move to Walberswick and we found a wonderful caravan and site there which we rented. We got jobs as waitresses in a restaurant by the front in Southwold and would cycle over the river everyday. It was quicker across the Bailey bridge by car. We had a lot of friends and I met my future partner there Paul Field. We were to set up home together in Bristol where I eventually went to university. He was a graduate from Hull University after getting his A-levels at Ipswich Tech and severely left wing.

Meantime at home Ruth my sister had persuaded the family we needed to move out of the family home and into this dark foreboding Elizabethan manor house on the top of the hill round the corner. Dad asked me "why didn't you help Mum move?" Apparently they took her there in a tractor and trailer. To this day when ever I dream of home I always dream about Bullocks Hill and not Hill house Farm which had no meaning for me.

So that was my gap year. Kathy wanted to go to America with me and work with the kids at Camp America and then travel round by greyhound bus. I turned her down. I was quite cruel to Kathy who was my best friend at school as my life was going in quite a different direction to where it had been. When I recovered years later I got in touch with her again but she died of non specific Hodgkinsons disease last year; 17th May 2008. She was a much blessed friend.

One wrong note

So the time came for me to go to Bristol, my third choice. I decided to go there as it was more integrated into the town than Brighton where I was also accepted (and Manchester). Also one of my sister's best friends Liz Jones was there and she showed me round. She was always incredibly kind to me throughout university.

I had a preview as all the crowd from Walberswick/Southwold were driving down to Cornwall for a sailing regatta. I hitched down on my own and bumped into them fortuitously filling up at a gas station in Penzance. The world was a small place in those days. I remember Paul Field was very keen to get into my tent. We went to Mousehole one night and I retained a love of the place returning when I was on the run from a mental hospital years later. It was just as magical.

Ann Lawson

From Cornwall I hitched up to Bristol and stayed with Liz and her boyfriend Austen Morgan an anarchist from Derry Northern Ireland. He is a distinguished barrister now but then he was in the hub of revolutionary politics. I smoked dope for the first time and heard the music. I wrote to Paul and got him to come and stay there. My life seemed to be going in a certain direction.

Mum drove me to my lodgings in Bristol. My head was all over the place after six hours in the car with her and it took me a long time to get my equilibrium back. I had changed subject from History and History of Art to Sociology and Politics, largely on Austen's advice. Plato was defeating me though.

I wrote regularly to Paul but was active in student politics too and went over to a Red Europe conference with Tariq Ali and his brother in law Andrew Shallice who was a student in my year and his friends Dave Prior and his wife. Liz and Austen also went.

Paul came to visit me in my lodgings and I decided to live with him so after living fairly roughly for quite a while we found a flat together and furnished it with anything we could salvage from charity shops and skips. The flat was on the top floor in Clifton with a view of the famous Suspension Bridge and the Avon Gorge.

My first essay for my sociology tutor, Huw Beynon, now a professor, was on the topic 'do you think society is a football team or 'them' and 'us?' I wrote an essay saying I believed it was 'them' and 'us.' Huw wrote in the margin 'who?' It was about the only comment he made and it jumped out at me and I just couldn't answer it. At school I had wanted to know everything and here on my first essay a simple question like that had completely floored me. Of course he was talking about the bourgeoisie and the proletariat but for me the question went much deeper.

I wrote to Mum and Dad giving my news and they were both very angry that I wasn't reading my intended subjects, history and history of art, and also living with Paul. I came top in my first year exams but I was beginning to suffer from depression and Paul was getting bored.

Only You Can Cure Yourself

I changed from joint honours sociology and politics to joint honours sociology and economic history to appease my parents. Paul decided to do a year's further education teacher training in London. So he helped me move into a shared house; the top two storeys in a beautiful terrace overlooking Bristol docks. I used to take the bus weekends to visit him. I worked very hard in my second year and was even writing off my own bat a research document on alienation. However real life stepped in. I asked Huw an innocent question in a tutorial and he blew me sky high. I think it was the first time I had opened my mouth. I cried and cried. One of his research students, Martyn was living in the same house as me and he explained a few things about Huw to me. We became very close and I became more and more attached to Martyn. One night after a party in the house when some dope was smoked, I walked into his room with only a blanket round me wanting answers to my confused mind but the obvious thing happened and we became lovers.

That night Martyn said "you remember the first and the last" I said "well my first was a French man, but that didn't matter, and I guess you are my last."

Paul was very angry and hurt when I told him, and Martyn already had another lover, and a girlfriend, who was imminently due back from Germany.

I went to the university GP for help but she just said "what do you expect if you sleep around."

Paul completed his course in London and I persuaded him to move with me into the flat below in the house I was living in already. I was very, very confused by this time. I wrote to my parents. The flat was beautiful with a long balcony overlooking the communal gardens. The owners of the house, who lived downstairs, had done it all up in 'Habitat' and there was a mezzanine floor over the kitchen and enormous folding wooden doors into the back bedroom.

I was really quite depressed by this time. Paul just laughed at me. Martyn and I were still occasional lovers. He was confused too.

One night when the flat was full to bursting with friends all partying, my mother arrived all the way from Suffolk. She stayed the night. So did everyone else. There were only two beds.

After Mum had gone, Paul stopped people coming round. He got a job in Bath teaching liberal studies in a further education college. But I couldn't study and panicked because my third and final year was coming up. So I left him; intending to live on my own. He cried and told me he loved me, and of course I loved him. He was my mother my father and my family to me. I called him my rock, but with Martyn I had discovered just how brilliant sex could be, as always after smoking dope. My parents found out later and were convinced the reason for my problems was because I "was on drugs at University."

I had made my mind up. I was going to move away from the mess and try and work it out in my own head. 'I wanted to be alone' a la Marlena Dietrich.

One wrong note

What actually happened was quite different to what I planned. Andrew Shallice, Tariq Ali's brother in law, heard I was looking for a new place and said he wanted to share. After much pavement pounding, I found a cold dirty basement in a house owned by an American Mathematics Professor. I have no memory of the address and despite being back to Bristol, can't find it. Andy, a friend of his called Sam Davies who is now a Professor of History in Liverpool and I moved in. Andy's parents came to visit shortly afterwards and I let them have my bedroom for the night whilst I shared Andy's room. After a late night walk we became lovers.

I felt like a complete tart but like the song decided I had to 'love the one you're with.' At first I cried so much Andy said he had never heard anyone cry like it. I used to walk the streets nearby at night. Martyn thought I was lonely. I was in a 9.00am history class in my final year. I told my history tutor that I was finding it difficult to work and when he asked about Andy I said, "I don't know him." He suggested I visit my sister who was living in York. So during that year I quite often travelled to York, working in the York University library. My parents came down to see me in Bristol and found me distraught. Later, Paul said, "When I found out that you were with Andy I decided it was all over, but it took a long time for me to get my confidence back."

I had been going to the University Socialist Society meetings every week and it had been my lifeline. Now a delegation came to the basement and begged me to be chair. However I felt I couldn't do it without Paul and turned them down. I bet you are getting as confused as I was by this time about who is who! Apparently everyone was talking about me.

I used to work at the makeshift desk I made and just couldn't stop taking pills, mostly aspirin. It became compulsive, as did smoking cigarettes, which had been under control before this. One day, after taking 10 aspirin, I walked down to the Bristol Royal infirmary and declared I had taken an overdose. They gave me an emetic and kept me in a few days. Andy came to see me. I watched the woman over the way die as they didn't pull the screens fast enough. A psychiatrist came to see me and asked if I wanted to go to a mental hospital. I said, "No" being well versed in how it was a last resort, and he said, "Why are you crying then?" Sometimes I used to wonder whether if I had gone into mental hospital then it might have been sorted out, but I doubt it. They only would have given me ECT. Also I wrote to my parents from hospital but never posted it.

After that I decided to just keep my head down and work. I got a degree; joint honours sociology and economic history class 2ii. I was very disappointed because I wanted to do research and couldn't without a 2i.

I was offered the opportunity of a job as an administrator of the Bristol Polytechnic but turned it down and left Bristol. My brother Roger came to pick me up.

After Bristol I went to stay with my sister in York and look for a job. She was doing research there and living with Julian, a social worker. They had a small terraced house. Andrew Shallice turned up out of the blue one day. We used to see each other on and off when I was up North. I got as job with something called 'Community Industry' in Leeds as a 'scheme consultant.' Basically I was shepherding a group of school leavers in job creation schemes as the career's office couldn't find them anything else. We decorated an old person's flat (quite garishly!), helped convert a beautiful old woollen mill into a museum, and helped run a playgroup in Chapeltown, the immigrant area. First I stayed on someone's floor and eventually found a very small flat. After work I used to feel quite lonely as I had no television, no radio and no telephone. The bathroom had two doors and I didn't know how to lock the other door so I never took a bath. But then like my Mum I am an excellent strip washer. Every morning I had a bowl of cornflakes. Lunchtime was a flask of soup and supper was invariably a pork chop and tinned peas. I went every where by bus or cycle or hitching. Most weekends I hitched to Bolton where Andy was living with Dave Prior and his wife. I bumped into Martyn and his girlfriend in Leeds one day and he came back to the flat with me. I loved him very much for many years and guess I still do a bit. But then I loved Paul too and Andy. Paul and I weren't in contact though and still aren't. I got friendly with another scheme consultant who was black who introduced me to his family, who worked for Dennis Healey in the Labour party, whom my Dad had known. He also took me to a black club in Chapeltown. It was all quite an eye opener for me. He asked me to share a flat with him. When I wrote to Andy about it he was cross. The next time I visited he told me "this bed was hot last night." So I left him. I thought he would come to Leeds and apologise, and make it up, but he never did.

One evening I bumped into a friend of Andy's I had met in Leeds and he came back to mine and we made love. He didn't come back to visit me for over two weeks so I decided to leave Leeds to teach him a lesson. Mum came to pick me up and I went back to live at Stradbroke in Suffolk. I realised immediately I had made a mistake.
I got a job at home as a receptionist at the local country club where I had worked as a teenager before my illness. Then I found I was pregnant. I heard the news about the Ripper in Leeds. His first killing was just round the corner from my old flat. Times were very dark indeed and I knew something was wrong. Life couldn't be this bad. The father wouldn't answer my letters. Secretly I was arranging an abortion. Mum read my correspondence and insisted I see the local GP who referred me to Dr Abel a psychiatrist whose daughter had been in my class at school. No way was I going to see him. So with my parent's permission I went to the Marie Stopes Clinic in

London and had counselling and a termination. They said "you will probably want another child."

I got a job as a social worker in Norwich, not because I wanted to - I wanted to go back up North - but because I was scared of my father. I moved into a nice flat in Norwich, which Mum insisted I share with someone who was the daughter of a friend of theirs - a probation officer of all people. The first week I was there I began to feel a bit better. However that weekend on my flatmates advice I went to visit my parents and on the Sunday their GP interviewed me and phoned Dad to have me admitted to "a nice little" mental hospital in Norwich. "You will have a roof over your head and regular meals" the doctor told me when I refused to go and Dad put me on the phone. They got to the point of threatening to send an ambulance and I thought, "What the hell, perhaps it will give me a chance to do a bit of sociological participant observation. My father, handing me a bottle of whisky, drove me there through thick fog.

I realised it was a complete dead end and only stayed a week. I went back to work as a social worker. One day my parents came to the flat with my two youngest brothers and told me my elder brother Roger, who was studying at Oxford, had killed himself. My sister later told me he had put a knife in his heart in the middle of the night. The date was the 31st January 1975. The GP wouldn't allow me to go to the funeral and I was driven back to the mental hospital, by my sister, immediately after it. I wandered the soulless corridors for four months, sewing stuffed frogs and reading about my brother's death as headlines in the local paper, which was left lying around. The food was mostly mashed potato and cold pilchards. Much later they tore this hospital down and I ransacked the empty shell collecting mementos, wandering through the doctor's offices which had been out of bounds and deliberately setting the fire alarm off, running off with my booty. This was whilst I was still ill.

My social work supervisor arranged for me to work as a care assistant in an old people's home in Norwich and eventually, caught between a rock and a hard place I decided to take the job. So I donned a char ladies overall and cleaned loos and emptied bedpans and made beds for a year. Then I discovered the probation officer I was sharing with was getting four times the amount of money I was and I was slogging my guts out at a job I hated. I was sacked and was delighted. I was riding high but, Mum insisted I see the psychiatrist again. We had the most terrible argument but she was adamant. The psychiatrist said I either go back into hospital or live at home. I chose to live at home.

I don't want to talk about that time much. Mum and Dad were still in grief. I was now in grief. I moved out for a while and stayed in Eye, the town, where I was born and worked as a personal assistant to the guinea fowl manager in a chicken processing co-operative. I sold the whole guinea fowl section to France by telex and my boss went too, so I was out of a job. Then I stayed in local cottages, one of which was Dad's and made a few friends but when my relationship with a student on the farm broke up I returned home. This student was related to my second brother's godmother and that brother's daughter has been ill like me.

I got madder and madder and more and more suicidal. I started running away - just walking out the gate and hitching God knows where. I slept with lorry drivers and worried a lot of people. I was in and out of a mental hospital in Ipswich, which I quite liked. There were arguments and lectures all the time from my parents and one night Dad even thumped me and made my nose bleed when I fell against the drinks cabinet.

I was in the habit of coming down and smoking the butt off one of Dad's cigars in the middle of the night when I was out of tobacco and couldn't sleep. One night there was no butt and I set light to the curtains with my lighter then ran outside onto the farm and put my lighter to the straw in the Dutch barn. I hid in the bales above the pigs in one of the pig houses. I had reached rock bottom. All night long I hallucinated. This was autumn 1978. Thatcher was shortly to be elected.

The police found me in the morning and after a drugged cup of coffee I was carried off in a strangle hold and taken to Ipswich where I was transferred to Rushmere Ward on Foxhall Road Ipswich, the so called violence ward of East Anglia. I discovered later there had been £70,000 of damage in the fire, most of which Dad got back in insurance.

Only You Can Cure Yourself

I was locked in a cell for several days with the window concealed by shutters. After a while they gave me a cardboard pot for my business and eventually a burly nurse took me out for a wash. I banged on the walls with my fists because I thought I would be in there for ever and they opened the door and asked what all the noise was. I said "music" lying.

After a while I was allowed freedom of the ward although it was locked at all times. I took my meals on the ward. There was mostly old ladies who had been there since having a "shock" on their wedding nights and women who had been admitted for having illegitimate children years ago, who were still shuffling about carrying dolls the nurses had given them instead. Some of them were tied to their chairs they were thought to be so violent. Probably their unpredictable movements were the result of long term heavy drug therapy -Tardive dyskinesia. It was an all - female ward but there was one male nurse who was also quite a bully. I read the Guardian and wrote letters to friends, which were all read by the nurses. I would eye the fire alarm looking to escape. I walked up and down the ward all day. I cried like a banshee for days. The doctor made me a cup of coffee and sat with me for a few minutes.

Eventually Mum and Dad were allowed to visit me. Dad said "think about the pigs." I didn't know any pigs had been killed until later. I didn't like thinking about the pigs.

Sometimes in the middle of the night I would have a cup of Horlicks with the nurses sitting round the gas fire.

The doctor came to see me every week. My parents had phoned Dr Abel the first psychiatrist in Norwich I had refused to see before the abortion and he suggested Broadmoor. I wrote to Mind and a lovely psychiatrist, Dr Fox, came down from Addenbrooks to give a second opinion. They gave me a year's section, - not my first section - and after four months with a little rehabilitation, mostly hands off bridge, I was back in the low secure hospital. The doctor said if I got a job and a place to live I could leave. So I did.

I lived in a shared house in Woodbridge and worked for an East Anglian company as a Personal Assistant to the managing director. I did that for a year; completed my section; then Mum and Dad came to visit and drove me to have an injection. The nurses said I need not have it if I didn't want to so I didn't and Dad was very cross (as usual). There was some interaction with my GP over sleeping pills and he felt I should go back to hospital so he drove me there and there I stayed for ages. It was obvious to me, Mum and Dad that it was the best place for me. Even the nurses were wondering why I stayed so long. In the end I was chatting to the receptionist at the hospital and she suggested Felixstowe was a nice place to live so I got a live-in hotel job in Felixstowe and moved out of the hospital. It was great to be by the sea again. I was as far away from my parents as I could manage. The job didn't last long. The proprietor said I was "too intelligent." It might have had more to do with spilling soup in someone's lap and keeping the bar open after hours.

I went to see the local social worker and was housed in a homeless unit with some teenage boys. I got another bar job. Then I moved in with one of the customers who was a chemical engineer working for Fisons.

I managed to get a job as a taxi driver. I don't think I was on medication at this time, which probably made it legal. It was a great job and I met loads of people and made loads of money. The engineer (who was an alcoholic) returned from being away one night and started banging my head against the skirting board. So I went out to my taxi and called Fox 13, which was the emergency call, just as he was about to punch me in the face. My boss turned up and took me to his place.

He was called Louis Woodhaddock. He had just taken over the company and was extremely disliked by the men. He immediately made me have an injection and then I soon realised he was as violent as my previous partner if not more so. He was living in a flat, in a hotel, which was crawling with cockroaches.

I found a flat and was going to move out but I needed Louis to act as guarantor and in the end decided to share with him. The extreme violence continued throughout our relationship. I would simply duck or curl up into a ball. I was too terrified to even think about striking back. At one time he wanted to buy a gun.

Only You Can Cure Yourself

My GP got pregnant and I had thought about having another child ever since the abortion so I went off my pills for about a week and found I was pregnant. I was very depressed at the thought but vowed to have the child and look after it for always. Maybe I thought I was ill because of the abortion and this would solve the problem. I had looked at a myriad of causes of my illness all the time never coming up with an answer. The morning of the fire, when I was carried off by the police, was the closest I ever got to the real truth. I tried to phone the family I had stayed with in France. My family never once told me the truth until I badgered them to death on the phone in 2002. I was dumbfounded and delighted when I discovered whom I had actually been staying with. My daughter is still caught up in the family of my youngest brother who lives exactly where the fire was and she has little to do with me. Perhaps that's why I don't want to talk much about that time. It was all chaos. My next book!

Louis continued his violence when I was pregnant. In fact when I gave birth I was covered in bruises where Louis had made violent love to me. Dad thought the nurses had been a bit rough. I did a lot of walking. Louis had another woman I discovered, so I went to the social worker and said "I am pregnant, Louis is violent and I have mental health problems can you re-house me." I think the only fact that registered was that I had mental health problems. They came round to the flat and assessed me and I had to show them my bruises. After a period in a bed and breakfast I was re-housed in a Cairn Gorm house which had been converted from the homeless hostel I had been in. There were three other families there with young children and babies. Louis found out where I was and came round and punched me in the face. When I went into labour I walked up to the phone box but it was out of order so I walked to another and called a taxi from Louis's firm. I was quite alone.

Tanya was born within 2 hours. The third of August 1982. I had wanted to call her Tristelle meaning a little piece of sadness from France but my sister had said no. Perhaps my illness would have been sorted sooner if I had. Anyway it is a beautiful name. She likes her second name though, Francella. Mum insisted she would be a Lawson and also that I spell Tanya with a 'y' not an 'I' as it looked better. When I was eventually allowed to leave hospital I went home for a week or so and Mum had made loads of preparations, including keeping all the cards I had received. But I couldn't wait to get back to being independent.

Our 'flat' consisted of one room near the docks, a gas fire, a sink, a stove and two bunk beds, a table and chairs. It was about 8' by 8'. There was a shared bathroom and stairs to the downstairs where we kept the prams. With a fridge, a deep freeze, a cot and a wardrobe, it was very crowded. After a year when Tanya was crawling I called the paper to take a photo of the place and a Tory councillor arranged for us to be re-housed in a two- bedroom council house nearby; 90 Coronation Drive, Felixstowe.

Tanya was a delight when she was small. Even the doctor said I was a good mother. I would walk her in her buggy along the sea front past all the fishermen. When I first moved into Coronation Drive I enjoyed every minute with her. I was devoted to her. The social worker Tony Bridges would come round regularly, as would the district nurse. Mum and Dad insisted I come home weekends as much as possible with her. Family and friends from the Stradbroke to Yugoslavia welcomed her arrival and sent cards and gifts. Many strangers gave small amounts of money for good luck; I put that money in a post office savings account for her. She was precious like all children.

Times were hairy though. One day the district nurse insisted I go to the surgery for some reason and from there they drove me to the Ipswich mental hospital. I was so disgusted I walked out but the nurses jumped on me and got me on the ground, they grabbed Tanya and took her off then carried me off. They stripped me and injected me and locked me in a side room. I escaped through a top vent somehow and walked across Ipswich in the dark with no shoes on to see Louis's mother to tell her what had happened. She allowed me to have a wash and gave me some cake then rather than call Louis, she called the police. I was kept in a secure hospital for six weeks whilst Tanya went to a foster home.

That was how Tanya was weaned off the breast and potty trained and took her first steps - whilst I was in a secure unit - with a foster mother who was a complete stranger. We were only reunited once I had signed to have a home help. But Tanya was traumatised as was

I. She would run off down the road constantly and I would have to run after her. It was exhausting and one day I just let her go and all hell let loose. She was only going to the swings and roundabouts behind the house anyway. The police were quite nice in those days.

Louis would come round and beat up anyone I dared to take up with and I would be wiping the blood off the walls.

I enjoyed my garden and the beach and decorating and improving the house. We had NO money except income support and family allowance. I knew a lot of people in Felixstowe from my taxiing days and there was generally a warm community surrounding us. It was a good solid house and in excellent order by the time I had finished with it. It was badly neglected when I first moved in. It would have been ideal to buy and I might have been very happy there if Dad hadn't been on to the social worker all the time stirring him up, so he would come round.

Louis tried to get custody of Tanya once he was convinced she was his, citing my mental health. He failed miserably and got two hours contact a month and an order to pay £4 a week.

One day my father turned up 'out of the blue' carrying a briefcase and wearing a suit. He said, "I'm going to buy you a house in Norwich, because you will never get rid of that man (Louis) and you will be nearer the family." It was a very, very cruel thing to do to Louis, for Tanya was his first daughter and he thought the world of her. But in my stupidity I agreed.

We lived at home in Stradbroke for a few weeks and it was a very happy time, whilst I travelled to Norwich to find a house. In the end I found a couple who were advertising in the paper for a council house exchange to Felixstowe and I liked them and their house so to preserve some independence from my family, I decided to move there. That was 15 Jessopp Road.

Not long after I had moved everything in and Tanya had arrived, we were playing out in the snow by the church opposite and a car drew up. In curiosity I went to see who it was and it was my parents. Dad sat on my phone all morning contacting doctors and mental health people to get me admitted to hospital and Mum took Tanya off.

From then on Norwich became the most depressing place on earth. I was put in Hellesdon Hospital and given massive amounts of drugs - Unbelievable amounts until I thought I would develop gangrene I was so immobile. All the patients took the mickey because I came from Suffolk. There was serious smoking going on and drugs and alcohol and the ward was dirty, deadly boring and unhealthy. We weren't allowed out for walks and nothing EVER happened. The psychiatrist spoke no English. There was no occupational therapy and there were a lot of institutionalised people wandering the grounds and buildings begging for dog-ends. It was disgusting. Even the food was disgusting. Moreover Dad, who had promised to look after Tanya, put her into foster care. There was absolutely no good reason for the hospital admission either.

Most mornings in Norwich I would wake up depressed. I missed the sea and the open space and my friends and Louis who was always in the background. Mum came up regularly but I dreaded her visits. I think they wanted a house in Norwich where Mum could eat her sandwiches after doing her shopping. The police in Norwich were vile too. I felt marooned, over medicated, bored, and disempowered. Tanya wanted to know when we were going home. She took to watching telly all day and that drove me nuts.

We had another blow up when she was due to go to school. I wanted to educate her at home as many people do. I didn't want her to become one of Thatcher's children. Dad blew the proverbial fuse and wrote to the chief education officer in Norwich. After a lot of argy bargy and a house siege by doctors and social workers (my youngest brother Robert was inside the house with me at the time) they put Tanya in foster care again to make sure she went to school. I wore out shoe leather getting a solicitor and eventually got her back, under a supervision order.

Things got worse and I began to lose my reason. I could see I would lose Tanya altogether if I wasn't careful. I phoned my tutor at Bristol Huw Beynon. I hadn't spoken to him since University and to my surprise he was kindness itself.

Shortly after that Dad bought 8 Buckingham Road and we moved in.

Only You Can Cure Yourself

After my marriage and Tanya going into care I started to get seriously ill. I missed Tanya terribly. She went to a good boarding school in Wymondham that took children in state care so she fared better than most. They had a very good music department. She wanted to do sociology, like her mother, but they couldn't timetable it, so she studied music. She had glandular fever but managed to get three A-levels and though she had said to me she didn't want to go to University, apparently a social worker sat her in front of a computer and she applied. She was one of the very few children in care who get to University. She was accepted at Manchester Metropolitan University to study for a four - year degree in teaching primary kids, specialising in Music. They realised she had dyslexia and gave her special help.

The social services went to court to prevent me having her address and I worried myself to such a point I thought she was dead and told someone so. I had always been worried she would commit suicide like Roger my brother.

Then she bought a house with her inheritance off Dad and the social services paid the mortgage. She was so pleased she invited me up and I went with Andy Reid my dentist friend from hospital.

She took five years to complete the course. She got a 2 ii like her mother.

Shortly after I recovered in 2002, when she was still on her course, the BBC asked her to be interviewed on breakfast television with a short film she had made about being in care. She wasn't keen to do it but I encouraged her and she had a whale of a time. She had left local authority care by this point.

Shortly after Jim left, and his kids had come round the house and beaten me up and robbed me, I took off by Eurostar to France. I was very confused and dazed, also having taken an overdose of Largactil. I was befriended by a young French man on a metro station, who was called Joel, because he was interested that I was reading a left wing French paper. I spent all night in Paris cafes with him until I felt safe enough to accept his invitation to stay with him and his mother for a while. His mother made me abundantly welcome and cooked fabulous meals. They lived in a small flat in the suburbs of Paris. We talked and talked and just clicked. I talked about losing my virginity in France, and about dad having a French mistress, and my illness. He told me about his mental illness. His father had worked in Paris but developed an industrial disease and moved out to the suburbs, hit the bottle and used to confide in Joel and also beat him up. He committed suicide. Joel felt 'la culpabilitee'; guilt.

We talked politics, philosophy, history and sociology. I mentioned that the son of the family de Broglie had stayed on the farm when I was young, and that they were very aristocratic, and he knew them immediately, as one had won the Nobel prize for physics on the wave nature of electrons (Louis de Broglie 1929) and they were a leading family in France. But I made no connection with the family I had stayed with in 1969.

I went to stay with Joel again and he came to stay here. I introduced him to my parents.

In 2001 I was in hospital under section as usual, for some forgotten reason, if there ever was one, and I saw the aeroplanes go into the twin towers on telly. I realised it was important and escaped and took the train to London then Bristol and went to visit my university friend Liz Jones. I had a bath and looked through the open window and felt the terrible menace in the skies. Liz found me a place in a homeless unit and then the police picked me up and I was brought back by car to Norwich from a mental hospital they had put me in. I was beginning to recover. I was determined. Tanya when she had been in care had concluded when she was in counselling that her main problem was that I didn't get on with my parents.

I think the authorities saw me as a lost cause by this time and I was alone in 8 Buckingham Road for quite a while and worked on that lead. I particularly narrowed it down to the period in France in 1969, which was so confusing. One phone call I made to Mum and Dad who must have been at their wit's end with the amount of time I was calling, I said, "it was only a job."

Mum came up to visit unexpectedly and said, "We were very upset that you thought it was only a job, that family was the de Broglie's."

Only You Can Cure Yourself

Augustin de Broglie had been one of my favourite students who stayed on the farm when I was young. We children teased him like hell because he claimed he was royalty ('Prince Augustin de Broglie.') We dropped wet nappies from the attic window onto his head. We dug holes in the garden for him to fall into and one time he was so cross he tried to throw me in the pond but I was too strong for him. Dad says he used to wipe his mouth with his bread at the table. I remember him biting into a raw egg in the caravan that stood on the farm. We went up the tennis courts in the village and I thought what a good tennis player he was, but Dad wasn't impressed. He showed us a photograph of some palace in Paris and pointed out his room. Dad was always making out we were just humble peasants, but of course Dad had been to Oxford and left to become a pilot in the war and Mum had been to University too.

Knowing now that I was staying with the de Broglie's, everything suddenly fell into place. I could see why I failed Oxbridge. I could see why the French family treated me so oddly. Moreover I could see that my parents were doing me a great favour and honour by arranging a holiday there prior to my Oxbridge entrance. I could see that they had never abandoned me. I could see that I wasn't just a work horse. I found love, respect, honour and happiness. I had found the missing piece of the jigsaw.

Before I was ill a friend of the family Ivor Keys who was a professor of music was listening to me playing Chopin's nocturne in e flat. He said, "There is just one wrong note." Mum said he had thought I would get a first at university. My sister got a first and a doctorate and a fellowship. I think Ivor would be very upset to have thought I deliberately had a mental illness because of one wrong note to please him for 33 years. But when I answered that question of Huw's, 'who?' finally with 'the de Broglie's' I knew I had come home. I think it is more descriptive to say I had a screw loose. How do you define that in mental health terms? What diagnosis accords with that?

I was talking to Joel on the phone last night. He said that there would be several branches of the family. The problem had been that I said to Mum, "They haven't sent the tickets yet and it's getting late." She said, "Their telephone number is in the book under 'de James'." So I phoned Pierre de James in Paris and he sent them. I never for the life of me (quite literally at the time) made the connection with de Broglie.

Life hasn't changed. I have changed. I am no longer mentally ill. I no longer think something is wrong. Now I am making visible progress. 7 years later I am off my injections and my mental health nurse is thrilled. I am still on a small amount of medication at night. My daughter has travelled the world, and has had one very good relationship and is now doing her final teaching qualifying year and living in a caravan in a country area of Essex. I have so many friends. I like 8 Buckingham Road now and it is feeling like home. I am active in the local community and in mental health service user representation. I have had a fun and happy relationship for three years. I am moving on all the time. Every so often I think how blessed I am to have recovered after so much misery for so many years. I'm not suicidal any more and I have quite a lot of respect coming my way. God is in his heaven even if he is prone to take short holidays. Life is a struggle but it is worth while now. I found the missing jigsaw piece. That'll do, that'll do.

Monday February 2, 2009 - 01:45pm

Where has winter gone?

I really haven't noticed winter this year. Everyone was complaining about the cold but I was fine. Perhaps it's because I went on holiday in October. I couldn't face another Christmas like the last one (Christmases are never the same anyway) but winter has flown by and now the birds are already singing. Chris and I are still talking and I am feeling much happier since Christmas. I am getting into reading and chatting on the computer and am back doing all the activities I was doing last year including being elected vice Chair of the service users council. We have the first committee meeting of the year of Friends of Eaton Park too on Thursday. I'm hoping to do some voluntary work too, serving teas and coffees in an old church up the town. My weight is going down with my new medication and I'm generally happy and optimistic again. I don't know what brought on my depression before Christmas, perhaps booking a holiday at the last minute and as a result missing so much, perhaps giving up smoking (and taking it up again). It doesn't matter; we all suffer from depression from time to time. But this is my favourite time of year. I have ordered some bulbs to be planted, already growing, in the area we have cleared at the bottom of the garden so they should make a lovely show this spring.

I listen to radio 3 a lot these days and I am reading Clare Tomalins biography of Samuel Pepys. I am enjoying both immensely. Last night I put the Enigma variations on which have a terrific brass element. Fortunately these houses are sound proofed and you can't hear from one to the other, anyway Maurice my neighbour is deaf.

My community psychiatric nurse wants to see me monthly to keep me on her caseload so we plan to go for a walk by the university. We call it 'dog muck alley' as so many people walk their dogs there, but it is a lovely spot in Earlham Park by the river Yare and near to the house Elizabeth Fry was brought up in. Then perhaps I'll have a swim afterwards in the sports centre and take the bus home.

My smoking really has gone down and I think the counsellor's advice last summer has stuck. Also now I hardly see Chris at all I am not influenced by his smoking (sorry Chris xx). I have a little Tardive dyskinesia I think from all the antipsychotics I have taken over the years but it doesn't trouble me and I just take a pill to counteract it if it does. It may just be a comfort thing anyway, my rocking.

Ruth has asked me to stay with her in New Zealand in her new house, but I am booked up for the moment and anyway, with the markets as they are, don't have the airfare.

I am going to stay with my friend Joel in Paris soon. He has had mental health problems since his father committed suicide. I met him when I was still ill. I was wandering around France after my divorce in a confused state. He and his mother were exceptionally kind to me.

Then in June I am doing a three day residential course in Oxford on the Abolition of Slavery. I shall use my disabled rail card to get down there. I was hoping to stay with Ann Cartwright, Mum's friend and a retired medical researcher and writer but she says she can't book up that far ahead. Apart from Mum and Dad I am feeling a bit ostracised by the family but I guess I wasn't in very good form towards the end of last year with Chris and I splitting up. Tanya my daughter has split up with her man too as has my sister Ruth with her partner so 'love is definitely NOT in the air!' However I still have a lot of terrific friends and am managing to occupy myself with my own company.

Mum seems a bit low now she can't drive but Dad is keeping his golf up despite looking after Mum and doing all the cooking as she isn't capable any more.

God bless any one who reads this.

If we didn't suffer we wouldn't know what happiness is.

Only You Can Cure Yourself

Wednesday January 28, 2009 - 07:41am

Mum
My Mother has been diagnosed with dementia.

Mum looked after me and my daughter for years when I was ill. She persevered even though I just wanted to continue my life without treatment. She knew there was something slightly wrong with me and she struggled for over thirty years to see me right. It wasn't till 2002 that I finally put in enough effort to find out what it was that would reunite us and Mum came up trumps.

I have loved and treasured her company since then. It hasn't been plain sailing for either of us. I continued to be hospitalised and treated like a loony by the authorities and it has been a major struggle to get back on my feet. Meanwhile Mum has had a small car accident and been treated for detached retinas which could have left her blind. She has been complaining about her brain for a long time now and she has always been kind of slightly confused and scatty (but very intelligent as I discovered.) Now it is confirmed and she is on medication.

She has a lovely happy disposition and enjoys company. However she has deteriorated a lot in the past few months. My sister stayed at home over Christmas and did a lot of looking after her and Dad...teaching Dad to cook. We are trying to get them more help in the house but just at the moment I am feeling I should do more. But

I live 50 miles away and the history of our association is still a bit of a bad memory from when they were trying to get me right.

I lost 30 years of my life being ill and that included 30 years of enjoying my parents. I feel it very strongly now Mum is ill. I could have done with knowing them longer. I am not much good at practical help but I would love just to go down there and show Mum some loving. God bless her! She did so much when I was ill.

Feeling better

A small miracle has happened over Christmas. I had had a really bad night because I was out of medication and left the phone off the hook and was really, really pissed of. Anyway my daughter must have phoned and was worried and called up the mental health services and insisted they do an assessment of me. So they phoned me and came round and later on delivered some sleeping pills to my house. I don't know how I would have got through the next night if Tanya hadn't helped so now I know she not only cares but is prepared to help, so my depression has lifted and I believe in God again. Bless her cotton socks...apparently she thought I had been angry with her. I was just hurt by what she had said. Anyway 'cool' is the word. I shall play it all very cool. She has had a tough time.

So One and All a Happy and successful New Year. God bless you all.

Thursday January 1, 2009 - 12:02pm

Chucked Chris

I have been miserable, totally, recently and Chris has given me zilch sex so finally I have chucked him. It doesn't make me feel any better but I am fed up with his abuse with no reward. God knows what will happen at Christmas now. I hate him

Only You Can Cure Yourself

Monday December 22, 2008 - 10:43am

Christmas

My sister is over from New Zealand for Christmas. She has been here a week and still not bothered to see me. In fact it is likely I won't see any of the family for Christmas. Still I had better drop all their presents off and all the food I have bought for them.

I have a cold which has gone to my chest.

I'm still getting no sex even though Chris is reasonably friendly on the phone.

My brothers are all off on Christmas holiday jamborees.

Tanya has totally cut off contact with me.

Hey ho what fun it is in the Lawson family.

Tuesday December 16, 2008 - 08:42pm

Off my injections!!!
Well I do have something to be cheerful about this Christmas after all. With the deep depression I have been in recently I decided I just couldn't take any more of the vile medication and with a little push from my brother and a little help from my father (and Chris!) I have finally persuaded the authorities I can take oral medication rather than monthly injections. That has taken me 30 years to achieve and you just can't believe what a bugbear of mine it has been. So I am ecstatic. Now I only have to take this one pill at night (and the other medication I have been taking) and I am free! I couldn't have done it without Chris supporting me, all through our relationship, to get a constant reduction in the injection and now I finally don't have that awful humiliation any more of a needle in the bum. That is real progress. I was so deeply ashamed about it I couldn't even bring myself to tell people, but my brother brought it out into the open and the rest followed. Now that really is the road to recovery. The previous time I saw the shrink she said it would be ten years if I

stayed out of hospital which is probably why I got so depressed. Now I hope Chris will recover from his man flu too. Adrian has asked me to his for a family Christmas with my parents and my sister and maybe my daughter so things are looking very good all of a sudden.

Confidentiality

We meet as service users once a month to discuss the hospital trusts policy yet because of issues of confidentiality, few of us have each others e mail or telephone which is an impossible way to work especially when the hospital has everyone's.

On the other hand the authorities are planning to publish our clinical notes, warts and all on the Internet whereas we have to pay £50 to see them ourselves. These are the notes written by every Tom, Dick and nutter who has ever had care of us.

I use the word care loosely as care really means being confined to an increasingly small space with heavy security, threats of worse and regular chemical gang rape by nurses. That's if they don't decide you need your brains burnt out and your memory destroyed by ECT.

I had a pre-meeting meeting with the chair and vice chairs today, I am to discuss the agenda with the authorities. Bugger me but the chair had invited this careerist service user with no elected authority to come along and tell us she thought none of us should be paid. The ruckus in a tiny room was enough to drive anyone to drink. It was supposed to be a quiet meeting where we got through the work quickly. As it was I threw a total wobbly and walked out. Now if we had had contact information I could have contacted her and the chair before hand to lodge my objections to an un-elected service user attending. However soon every employer and insurance agency will be able to look up on the net just what I got up to 30 years ago in some forgotten and probably destroyed mental asylum across the country and hold it against me.

Only You Can Cure Yourself

Tuesday May 19, 2009 - 05:34pm

Getting back into the flow of things

I've done pretty well the last few days. I have achieved a few things. It helps now I go to Church; it gives me a good framework for my life and it is enjoyable and thought provoking.

I have several conferences coming up so I've bought some clothes mail order as I've been delving the depths for things to wear recently.

I've written to my daughter's father in America to see if we can organise Tanya meeting him. She last saw him before she was 3 and doesn't remember him, though they do write to each other sometimes.

Monday May 18, 2009 - 11:39am

Indolence

I have been a bit dreamy since coming back from France, missing important appointments and generally wafting around at home rather than getting on with things. I really must start applying my self again; I'm getting into lazy ways and that is ultimately very unsatisfying. I've let several people down and argued with several more. Its very self-indulgent behaviour and I'm not very proud of myself. So I hereby resolve at 3.00 am (!) to pull my socks up and fulfil my obligations. At least I hope I can or I'll be back in the bin.

It was very interesting going to France but in the end Joel knows me from a time when I was very ill and it is difficult to change people's perceptions of oneself. I am a much more responsible person now but at the moment it is not showing. I feel very bad to have retreated into a comfort zone of my house, which in the end will take me no where. I must do what I say I am going to do.

I have been thinking about everything but getting on with life and you have to make do with what you have; it's no good just dreaming of what might have been. Whether I can stop letting things slide or not, I don't know. I do know it will make me ill if I carry on this way.

Friday May 15, 2009 - 07:09pm

Spring in my back garden

My garden is lovely at the moment but the birds are quiet as they are nesting

Only You Can Cure Yourself

Tuesday May 12, 2009 - 05:16am

Versailles

This is Joel, my friend and I in the Hall of Mirrors Versailles Paris this April

Seven years continual recovery after 30 years of mental illness

Leeds where I worked for a year after university

When I left Leeds and came home I knew I was heading for a deep dark tunnel. What I didn't know was just how long it would take to come out of it. I was pregnant at the time but didn't know. I aborted that child.

Wednesday May 20, 2009 - 01:31pm

St Stephens Church

This is the room where I help serve tea and coffees every Thursday morning

Only You Can Cure Yourself

Clifton Suspension Bridge

Bristol where I lived and studied for three years

Tuesday May 19, 2009 - 07:41pm

This is what confidentiality means:

Proposed Oregon bill would ease privacy laws on 3,600 cremains in canisters
The director of medical records at the Oregon State Hospital examines one of the more than 3,000 urns containing the unclaimed ashes of deceased patients.
Oregon's state-run mental hospital is famous as the place where 'One Flew Over The Cuckoo's Nest' was filmed. But there is another sad side to the crumbling old hospital, one that's fact, not fiction. From the early 1900s to the 1970s, the unclaimed bodies of 3,600 mental patients were cremated, and the remains were put in copper canisters and placed in storage.

Deciding that the remains deserve more dignified treatment, state officials have been trying to find relatives of the patients. But they have been hindered by privacy laws that protect patient's rights, even after they are long dead.

Perhaps this book will go some way to being a memorial to my wasted life and there will be something to show for it.

Men

I have decided not to look for another man. Joel gave me a good talking to in Paris and said I must cut from Chris, which I have done though we still chat sometimes. However I think my need to always have a man was part of my illness. I didn't trust my family and parents enough to look after me. When I was in France when I first got ill I turned to a man for comfort after I felt my parents had failed me. I have continued to do that for years now with all the heartbreak and compromise it entails. However going out with Chris I often felt

I was not giving my parents the support they needed. In fact our tiff after going to Ireland at Christmas was because I would have preferred to spend Christmas with my parents and I still feel bad about it. My family need me and also I can be myself, work better and concentrate better on my own. I have lots of friends and work commitments and I am perfectly happy without Chris; in fact happier now. I just feel a bit stupid that it took so long for me to chuck him proper. But I am not going to step into another relationship as I planned. If in the unlikely event an interesting one comes up then I might. However I have plenty to occupy myself without a man. I thought I wouldn't be able to manage without sex, which is why I took up with Chris. However I am managing fine.

I am in recovery, not recovered and it is a learning curve. I feel it was a big mistake on my part and has caused a lot of damage to everyone that I was so dependent on Chris for so long. We remain good friends and I like him but from now on I'll make my own decisions and do my own thing until if by chance I meet someone I want to marry etc. or at least someone in that category. I never would have married Chris though I did get sentimental at times. I feel rather foolish and very guilty that I let it drag on as I did but without my friend Joel's advice it would have carried on longer. Friends are invaluable for talking things through. Now I have a lot of work restoring faith.

Thursday June 4, 2009 - 11:22pm

Mental Health Cruelty

These days if you are not 'compliant' with your medication the authorities look for your weakest spot and threaten you unless you take it. For me it was my driving license as all my family live in Suffolk and are only accessible by car so they took away my license repeatedly so I couldn't see my elderly parents or brothers, sisters and nieces even at Christmas, our traditional time of get together. They went to extreme lengths to make sure I was drugged up. Fortunately I am on a low dose now and it doesn't make you eat constantly so I take it. However they were not in the slightest interested that I felt better at long last. The only thing they were interested in was that I be utterly compliant.

What brings this to mind is that at the service users council yesterday, a friend who has just got married and had a baby is being forced to take medication which is making her increasingly fat or they will take her baby away as they did her other children. She's a bright, intelligent girl and was obviously very pretty at one time but the medication is ruining her. As she says 'they have me over a barrel.' Even if you are suffering from cancer and will die without chemotherapy, no one can force you to take it.

How would you feel if your freewill was so cruelly denied? But the essence of mental health treatment is that the doctors are always right and you must negate yourself in their superior knowledge. However there is no claim the medication will cure you; it just blocks out reality. I have told them time and time again I can cope with reality and like myself but they are totally unmoveable. It is a civil liberties and human rights issue.

Most of the medication has horrible side effects; in fact the only aspect of it is the side effects as there is no evidence it is doing you good. Moreover the doctors insist on giving you such high doses that it is often quite impossible to live with. Then the threats they make (and carry out) if you don't take it are anti-therapeutic in the extreme. Psychiatry is rubbish. You need your head examining if you consult a psychiatrist willingly. It's a massive form of social control and social repression that is extremely long term and carries a message of severe 'no hope' to all who it encounters. Remember this and you will understand mental illness better.

Felixstowe

This is probably the exact bench where I decided to leave Louis
when I was pregnant with Tanya